Sugar Flowers

For All Seasons

Sugar Flowers

For All Seasons

Alan Dunn

MEREHURST

Dedicated with love to my parents, Allen and Avril; to my sister, Susan; and to my part-time partner in sugar-crime, Tombi.

ACKNOWLEDGEMENTS

First published 1996 by
Merehurst Limited
Ferry House,
51–57 Lacy Road,
Putney,
London SW15 1PR

Copyright
© Merehurst Limited 1996
ISBN 1-85391-503-3(hardback)
ISBN 1-85391-690-0(paperback)

A catalogue record for this book is available from the British Library.

Editor: Helen Southall
Design: Anita Ruddell
Photography by Sue Atkinson

Colour separation by P & W Graphics Pte Ltd, Singapore
Printed in China by
Leefung Asco

I would like to thank the following people, some for their direct help with this book, and others for their indirect help, support and, most importantly, their friendship before, during and after the writing of this book:
Alice Christie, Peggy Green, Maria Harrison, Margaret Morland, Sandra Robertson, Stephanie Scott, Viv Soulsby, Peter Stott and Tony Warren; Joan Mooney of Great Impressions, Sally Harris of Tinkertech Two, Norma Laver and Jenny Walker of A Piece of Cake, David and Margaret Ford of Celcakes, everyone at Cooks Corner, and Beverley Dutton of Squires Kitchen. Thank you also to Annemieke Mein for allowing me to use the Frog Down Under design, and to Rosemary Macdonald for the witch hazel and Caroline Goodrick for the silk.

An extra special thanks must go to Tombi Peck, without whose help this book would not have been finished in time, and I certainly would not have had so much fun during one very hot summer!

The author and publishers would also like to thank the following suppliers:
Anniversary House (Cake Decorations) Ltd., Unit 5a, Roundways, Elliott Road, Bournemouth BH11 8JJ; A Piece of Cake, 18 Upper High Street, Thame, Oxon OX9 3EX; Cake Art Ltd., Venture Way, Crown Estate, Priorswood, Taunton TA2 8DE; Celcakes and Celcrafts, Springfield House, Gate Helmsley, York, North Yorkshire YO4 3EX; Cooks Corner, 35 Percy Street, Newcastle-upon-Tyne, Tyne & Wear; Creating Cakes, 63 East Street, Sittingbourne, Kent ME10 4BQ; Great Impressions, Greenlea, 14 Studley Drive, Swarland, Morpeth, Northumberland NE65 9JT; Guy, Paul and Co. Ltd., Unit B4, Foundry Way, Little End Road, Eaton Socon, Cambs. PE19 3JH; W. Robertson, The Brambles, Ryton, Tyne & Wear NE40 3AN; Squires Kitchen, Squires House, 3 Waverley Lane, Farnham, Surrey GU9 8BB; Tinkertech Two, 40 langdon Road, Parkstone, Poole, Dorset BH14 9EH.

Contents

Introduction

When I first started decorating cakes, at the age of fourteen, flowers formed only part of the cakes' decorations, and my early floral efforts, made from sugarpaste, bore little resemblance to the real thing. After I was introduced to fine wired flowers, however, my ideas changed and flowers are now the main feature of my work.

Although I have had an interest in fresh flowers from an early age (I can remember quite clearly picking and collecting flowers, only to turn around and find that my two-year-old sister had plucked their heads off!), my love, fascination and appreciation for them has grown enormously in recent years. Now I am constantly in search of new and unusual flowers and foliage to copy in sugar, but sometimes I get so carried away with my admiration for the real thing that I don't get a sugar version finished! However, this all adds to the pleasure I get from my work. If I find an unusual flower to copy, I always make notes and templates in case I want to make the flower again at a later date and cannot find another specimen.

The flowers and foliage featured in this book are arranged into four sections – Florists' Flowers, Exotic Flowers, Garden Flowers and Wild Flowers – and each section includes some of my favourites from each season of the year. Although the flowers might appear very realistic, some of them only resemble the real thing and are not intended to be exact copies. In some cases, this is because the flowers were not in season at the time I needed to make them for the book (May to August 1995), and were therefore not available to copy. In any case, I feel it is more important to create the character of a plant or flower in a decorative display, rather than to strive for botanical correctness. It is also important to give your work soul; if a flower has been copied too closely and is too neat in form, the result can often look very sterile and lifeless. Most of all, it is important to enjoy what you are doing and to have fun when making sugar flowers!

M any of the cake designs in this book feature quite large bouquets and arrangements. I am very much inspired by the work of flower arrangers and florists, whose work tends to be on a large scale. Moreover, wedding cakes can often go unnoticed at a reception if the floral displays are small, especially if the reception is held in a large hall or room, so I tend to favour large displays. However, the instructions can easily be adapted to smaller arrangements, and I hope that this book will inspire you to develop your own ideas, making use of a selection of the flowers featured to suit your own personal taste and style.

Alan Dunn

Equipment & Techniques

Equipment

To make the sugar flowers and foliage in this book you will need the basic equipment listed here. Details of other items needed to make specific flowers are given with each set of instructions. Most of the equipment is available from specialist cake decorating suppliers.

BOARD AND ROLLING PIN

A non-stick board and rolling pin are essential for rolling out paste without it sticking. Grooved boards and rolling pins are very useful for creating thick central ridges on petals and leaves to allow wires to be inserted (see page 10). These are available commercially, but you can also make grooves yourself in the back of a non-stick board. To do this, heat a metal skewer until it turns red hot, and then brand the back of the board several times until you have achieved a groove of the required depth and width. (Several grooves of varied lengths and depths are useful.) Scrape off the excess plastic, and then smooth the board with some fine glass paper.

MEXICAN HAT BOARD

This board has holes in it of various sizes and depths and can be used for rolling out paste when a thicker central area is required. Start by rolling out some paste quite thickly, and then roll it out over the required hole until the surface paste is thin enough. Remove the paste from the board and you will be left with a thick area in the centre. This forms the back of a flower or the ovary on a calyx.

DRESDEN TOOL

This modelling tool can be used to create several different effects. The fine end of the tool is excellent for drawing veins down the centre of petals, calyx sepals and leaves, while the broad end can be used to draw veins on large pieces and to hollow out the inner edges and the centres of petals, sepals and leaves. The broad end is also used to create an effect known as 'double frilling'. This technique can give a 'ridged look' and, if worked to a certain degree, is ideal for creating jagged or ragged edges to leaves and petals. To create double frilling, press the broad end of the tool on to the paste and then drag it down against the board. Repeat the process many times until you have frilled the required area.

BONE-END TOOL

This is used to soften and gently frill the edges of petals and leaves. To use this tool place the petal or leaf on a pad and place the required end of the tool half on the paste and half on the pad. (For larger pieces, choose the larger end of the tool, saving the finer end for smaller pieces.)

Use long, strong strokes on the edge, repeating until you have the desired effect. This tool can also be used for cupping and hollowing out petals.

CELSTICKS

These are available in four sizes: small, medium, large and extra large. One end of each tool is pointed; the other is rounded. The pointed end is used to open up the centres of flowers and can be used for veining. The rounded end can be used like the bone-end tool, but with celsticks you have the advantage of a range of different-sized tools for various-sized flowers and leaves. The central part of a celstick is also regularly used as a miniature rolling pin.

PLIERS AND WIRE CUTTERS

Small fine-nosed pliers are essential, but they are expensive and an item to be treasured! I bought mine from an electrical supply shop. Wire cutters are also very useful; although scissors can be used, wire can ruin them.

FLORISTRY TAPE

Paper floristry tape is available in many colours but I use mainly pale green, white, beige and brown. The tape has a glue in it that is released when the paper is stretched, so it is important to stretch the tape firmly as you tape over a wire.

TAPE SHREDDER

This is used to cut lengths of floristry tape into various widths. If you remove one of the blades you will have a shredder that will cut one half- and two quarter-width lengths at the same time. The blades will need to be replaced from time to time.

WIRES

Various coloured wires are available in many thicknesses, from 14-gauge (thick) to 33-gauge (very fine). The quality of the wires available also varies; although expensive, it is best to buy A-grade wire. I use mainly white wires, preferring to tape over the stems when the flower is complete.

GREAT IMPRESSIONS (GI) VEINERS

These are double-sided rubber veiners moulded from real flowers and foliage. They add a great deal of realism to flower work. Once you have cut out your leaf or petal and inserted a wire (see page 10), place the shape into the veiner (the ridge on the paste should fit into the central vein on the back piece of the veiner). Press the two sides together firmly and then remove the leaf, now veined on both sides to natural perfection.

CERAMIC SILK VEINING TOOL

This tool has veins on the surface; when rolled over the paste it gives a delicate texture.

CUTTERS

There are many different types of cutters available on the market. I use mainly metal cutters as there are more shapes available, although I also have a large collection of plastic cutters. Cutters speed up the flower-making process and help to add consistency and accuracy to your work.

THREAD

Fine white lace-making thread (brock 120) is best used for stamens, although some thicker cotton threads can also be useful. Silk is used to make the Old man's beard seed-heads (see page 131). It is available from specialist lace-making shops.

PADS

These are firm pieces of foam-like material and are commercially available. They are used to hold paste while you soften or vein a petal or leaf.

PAINTBRUSHES

Good brushes are essential. They are one of the most important items in a flower-maker's tool kit. Remember that the final control and accuracy with colouring can make or break your work! Flat brushes are most useful for dusting flowers and foliage (round brushes are not firm enough to colour accurately with petal dust/blossom tint). I use mainly ¼-inch and ½-inch sable/synthetic flat brushes (such as Windsor and Newton series 606). You will also need a good selection of finer brushes for painting details on to petals and foliage.

Techniques

WIRING LEAVES AND PETALS

Roll out some flower paste to the required thickness using a grooved board or rolling pin. Remove the paste from the board and turn it over, if necessary, so that the ridge in the paste is on top. Cut out the shape, positioning the cutter so that the ridge of paste runs from tip to base of the leaf or petal. Press firmly, then release the paste from the cutter. Moisten the end of a wire and insert it into the thick ridge, holding the paste firmly between your finger and thumb to prevent the end of the wire coming through. Insert the wire into at least half the length of the ridge.

COLOURING

I use a small selection of paste food colourings to colour flower paste, preferring to alter and colour the flowers and foliage with petal dusts (blossom tints) after shaping. Petal dusts can also be mixed into flower paste to colour it, but if used in large proportions they can alter the consistency too much. I usually colour the paste a paler shade than I want the finished flower to be, and then dust on top to obtain more depth and realistic effects. It is important to have a good selection of petal dust colours and to experiment with different combinations to achieve the effect you want. I very rarely use one colour by itself. The instructions for each of the flowers in this book include a list of the colours used. One of the colours I use frequently is a dark green mixture which adds a lot of depth to foliage. To achieve the depth of green required, mix equal proportions of moss green and jade together, and then darken with nutkin and a little black.

GLAZING

In this book I have used two methods for glazing flowers and leaves. The steaming method is used to give a flower a slightly 'waxy' finish or simply to remove its dusty appearance. It is also used when you want to darken the colour of a flower or leaf, since the surface of the piece will accept more colour if redusted when it is still slightly damp after steaming. Hold each flower or leaf in the steam from a boiling kettle for a few seconds, until the surface turns shiny. Take great care as too much steam can soften and dissolve the sugar.

For a more permanent and shiny glaze, use confectioners' varnish. Used neat (full glaze), this gives a very high gloss, which is ideal for berries and glossy leaves. However, for most foliage this looks too severe, so it is better to dilute the varnish with iso-propyl alcohol (available from chemists; although vodka or other high-proof alcohols can be used, sometimes there is a reaction and a jelly-like substance is formed, so it is easier and cheaper to use iso-propyl). Place the varnish and alcohol in a lidded container and shake to mix. The glaze can be used straight away. Simply dip the leaf or petal (or a group of pieces) into the glaze, shake off the excess and dry on absorbent kitchen paper. It is important to shake the glaze in its container from time to time to prevent separation. The glaze can be applied with a paintbrush, but I find the brush strokes tend to remove the colour. The following glazes are those that I use most often.

¼ glaze
Three-quarters alcohol to a quarter part varnish. This is used for leaves that don't have much shine; the glaze just takes away the flat, dusty look of a leaf or petal.

½ glaze
Equal proportions of alcohol and varnish. This gives a natural shine that is ideal for many foliages, including rose leaves.

¾ glaze
Quarter part alcohol to three-quarters varnish. This gives a semi-gloss without the 'plastic' appearance of a full glaze.

USING A 'CAGE'

A wire 'cage' is used to mark the impression of unopened petals on a bud. The 'cage' is made from wire, the gauge depending on the size of the bud. If you are making the bud of a five-petalled flower, you will need five pieces of wire for the 'cage'. Tape the pieces of wire together at one end with

½-width floristry tape and open up the 'cage', trying not to cross the wires at the base. Insert your modelled bud, tip or base first depending on the effect required, and close the wires on to its surface, keeping them as evenly spaced as possible. For some buds, a more realistic effect is achieved if the paste between the wires is pinched out and thinned with your finger and thumb to form a ridge that gives the appearance of larger petals. After removing the bud from the 'cage', twist the petals to give a spiral effect.

MAKING FLOWER PASTE

The type of flower paste used is a matter of personal choice. I prefer a paste that stretches well and does not dry out too fast. I always buy (by mail order) ready-made-up flower paste because it is more consistent than home-made paste and it saves me a lot of time and trouble. You can make your own from the following if you wish.

5 teaspoons cold water
2 teaspoons powdered gelatine
500g (1lb/3 cups) icing (confectioners') sugar, sifted
3 teaspoons gum tragacanth
2 teaspoons liquid glucose
3 teaspoons white vegetable fat (shortening) or 2 teaspoons soya oil
1 egg white (size 2)

1 Mix the cold water and gelatine together in a small heatproof bowl and leave to stand for 30 minutes. Sift the icing sugar and gum tragacanth into the bowl of a heavy-duty mixer and fit the bowl to the machine.

2 Place the bowl with the gelatine mixture over a saucepan of hot water and stir until the gelatine has dissolved. Warm a teaspoon in hot water and then measure out the liquid glucose (the heat should help to ease the glucose off the spoon). Add the glucose and white fat or soya oil to the gelatine mixture, and continue to heat until all the ingredients have dissolved and are thoroughly mixed together.

3 Add the dissolved mixture to the icing sugar with the egg white. Fit the beater to the machine and turn the mixture on at its lowest speed. Beat until all the ingredients are mixed, then increase the speed to maximum until the paste is white and stringy.

4 Remove the paste from the bowl and rub a thin layer of white fat over it (to prevent the outer part drying out). Place in a plastic bag and store in an airtight container. Allow the paste to rest and mature for at least 12 hours before using it.

IDENTIFYING THE PARTS OF A FLOWER

Throughout this book, reference is made to the various parts of a flower. The illustration and following notes will help you identify them.

Pistil
The pistil is the female part of the flower and is made up of stigma, style and ovary. In many flowers, e.g. a lily, this piece can be quite large.

Stamens
The stamens are the male part of the flower and are made up of a filament and a pollen-covered anther. In order for a flower to be pollinated, the pollen must be transferred to the stigma on the pistil. Once a flower has been pollinated the ovary will start to grow and, in some cases, fruit will form.

Petals
These are the most attractive, coloured parts of a flower, their main purpose being to attract insects to the flower.

Tepals
These look like petals and appear in flowers that have no calyx, e.g. lily, anemone or Christmas rose.

Calyx and sepals
The calyx is made up of separate sepals. It is the outer layer of a bud that protects the flower while it is forming inside.

Bract
This is located where the flower stem joins the main stem. It is a small, modified leaf (intermediate between the sepals and the leaves).

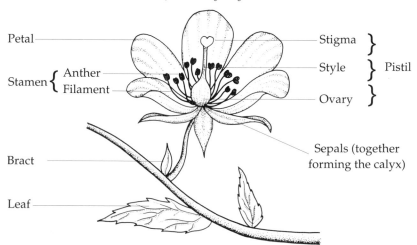

The parts of a flower

Petal —
Stamen { Anther — Filament —
Bract —
Leaf —
Stigma }
Style } Pistil
Ovary }
Sepals (together forming the calyx)

Florists' Flowers

𝒯HIS SECTION IS PROBABLY the
most useful for sugarcrafters, as these are
the flowers most frequently given as gifts
for birthdays, anniversaries, mother's day,
etc., and, most importantly, are those used
in bridal bouquets and arrangements. I
visit flower shops on a regular basis, in the
hope of finding something unusual and
exciting to inspire me.

Rose

The rose *(Rosa)* is still by far the
most popular flower, and many hybrids
are available from florists all year round.

wanted the finished flower to be
quite dark, I started with a paler
base. For white roses, add a tiny
amount of melon or bitter
lemon colouring to give the finished flowers their characteristic
warm glow or green tinge.

FIRST AND SECOND LAYERS

3 Roll out some coloured
flower paste fairly thinly,
and cut out four petals using the
smaller cutter (551). Place the
petals on a pad and soften the
edges with the rounded end of a
large celstick, working half on
the paste and half on the pad.

PREPARATION

1 Roll a ball of white flower
paste into a cone with a
sharp point and a fairly broad
base (it should be no larger than
the small petal cutter you are
planning to use; for a bud it
should be quite a lot smaller).
Tape over an 18-gauge wire and

bend an open hook in the end.
Moisten the wire and insert it
into the base of the cone, making sure that the hook goes
almost to the tip. Pinch the base
of the cone firmly on to the wire
to secure. Make as many as you
need and allow to dry
overnight.

2 Colour some flower paste as
required. I have used ruby
paste colouring and, although I

4 Moisten the central part of a
petal and place it on a dried
cone, leaving about 5mm (¼ in)
of the petal above the tip of the
cone. Tuck one side of the petal

in towards the cone (you are aiming to hide the tip of the cone completely), and wrap the other side of the petal around to form a tight spiral, leaving the end slightly open. (Do not worry about the base of the cone at this stage.)

5 Moisten the bases of the remaining three petals. Tuck the first of these underneath the edge of the petal on the cone, the second underneath the first and the third underneath the second. The petals should now be fairly evenly spaced. Moisten the petals a little more if needed and close them all tight, pulling the petals down at an angle rather than wrapping them straight around. There are now enough petals on to make a small bud, but if you are planning to make a larger rose, open up one of the petals again.

THIRD AND FOURTH LAYERS

6 Roll out some more paste and cut out another three petals with the same cutter (551). Vein the petals, if you wish, using either the ceramic tool or the double-sided veiner (some roses have a texture, others do not; decide which you prefer). Soften the

edges as before. Start again by tucking the first petal of the third layer underneath the last petal of the second layer. Continue to add the remaining petals as before, this time pinching a very gentle central vein on each of the petals between your finger and thumb as you add them to the rose.

7 Cut out another three petals and repeat step 6, this time wrapping the petals less tightly to give a more open appearance.

FIFTH AND SIXTH LAYERS

8 Roll out some more paste and cut out another three petals using either the same size cutter as before or the next size (550), depending upon how large the rose has already become. Vein and soften as before. This time you will need to cup the centre of each petal, using a large celstick.

9 Moisten the base of each petal and attach them as before, making sure that the centre of each covers a join on the previous layer. The rose should now be quite open; curl back the edges of each petal using your fingers or a cocktail stick (toothpick). At this stage, the rose is termed a 'half rose'; I usually use more half roses than full ones in a spray or bouquet.

10 Roll out yet more paste and cut out five petals using the larger cutter (550). Vein, soften and cup each petal, and moisten the base edge. Place the first petal over a join on the previous layer, and place the second petal over another join on the opposite side of the rose. Place the third petal over the join (or gap) created by the previous two, and the last two next to each other, covering the large space on the other side of the rose. Curl back the edges of each petal as before, and, if you have damaged the cupped shape of the petals, place the broad end of a dresden tool down the centre of each to re-form. A few more smaller petals can be added if the rose looks unbalanced at this stage.

11 If you are working on a pale coloured or white rose, it looks attractive if you dust the inside of the base of each petal lightly with a mixture of primrose, lemon and white petal dust. It is easier to do this while the flower is still soft. Dust the outer petals of a bud, half rose or full rose at the base with the same colour. The roses illustrated have been dusted with fuchsia and plum petal dusts, and then over-dusted with aubergine.

CALYX

12 Roll a ball of mid-green flower paste into a cone and pinch out the base to form a hat shape. Using a small celstick, roll out the base to make it a little thinner, although the calyx should have quite a 'fleshy' appearance. Cut out the calyx, and elongate each of the sepals by rolling over with the celstick.

13 Place the calyx on a pad and cup each sepal on the inside. Dust the inside of the calyx with a mixture of white and moss green petal dust to make it paler. If you wish, you can make some fine cuts in the edges of each sepal with a pair of fine scissors, to give them a 'hairy' appearance.

14 Moisten the centre of the calyx and attach it to the back of the rose or bud, trying to position each sepal so that it covers a join between two outer petals. On a full-blown rose, the calyx would curl back, but position it tightly around a bud. Dust with moss and dark green.

LEAVES

15 Rose leaves can grow in groups of three or five, depending upon the variety. Roll out some mid-green paste using a grooved rolling pin or board. Remove the paste from the groove and cut out a selection of sizes using rose leaf cutters. You will need one large, two medium and two small leaves per stem.

16 Choose lengths of 26-gauge or 28-gauge wire (depending on the size of leaf) and cut into four. Moisten one end of each wire and insert into

the thick ridge of a leaf. The wire should be inserted into at least half the length of the leaf. Vein the leaf using the double-sided veiner. Place the leaf on a pad and soften the edges using a large celstick. Pinch a vein down the centre, and shape the leaf between your finger and thumb to give a little movement.

17 Dust the back of each leaf with white and a little moss green petal dust. Over-dust with aubergine/plum on the edges. Turn the leaf over and dust the edges with aubergine/plum, making the colour heavier on one side. Dust the main part of each leaf with dark green and then over-dust with holly/ivy. Glaze using ½ glaze.

ASSEMBLY

18 Tape the leaves together into groups of three or five, starting with a large leaf, then medium, and finishing with small leaves. Dust the stem with a little dark green, holly/ivy, aubergine and plum.

Stargazer Lily

There are many species of Oriental lily *(Lilium)* and most of those we buy from flower shops are hybrids. The 'Stargazer' hybrids are large, colourful flowers with an exquisite scent, making them ideal for bridal bouquets.

Materials

18, 24 and 26-gauge wires
Fuchsia, plum, red, moss, dark green, skintone, primrose, aubergine and deep purple petal dust (blossom tint)
Ivory, pale holly/ivy and mid-holly/ivy flower paste
Semolina
½ glaze (see page 10)
Cyclamen liquid colouring

Equipment

Fine pliers
White and pale green floristry tape
Lily cutters or templates
Casablanca lily veiners (GI)

STAMENS

1 Use a third of a length of 26-gauge wire for each stamen. Using fine pliers, bend a flat hook in one end of each, then hold the hook halfway down with the pliers and bend it again to form a 'T'-bar. The filaments are very fleshy in this lily so thicken them with several layers of ¼-width white floristry tape. Dust the tape with a mixture of primrose and moss green petal dust.

2 Attach a sausage of ivory flower paste over the 'T'-bar to form the anther, bending both ends down so that it resembles a moustache. To make pollen, mix a little semolina with some skintone petal dust. Moisten the anthers and dip into the pollen mixture. Allow to dry thoroughly. (Florists usually trim off the anthers as the pollen can stain fabric very badly, especially bridal gowns! Nevertheless, I still prefer to make the flower with them.)

PISTIL

3 Form a ball of pale holly/ivy flower paste and insert a moistened 24-gauge wire. Work the paste between your finger and thumb in a rubbing motion, and try to cover a good length of the wire. (The pistil should measure at least the length of one of the petals.) Smooth the pistil between the palms of your hands and trim away any excess paste. Flatten the top of the pistil with your finger, and then, using a pair of tweezers, pinch the end into three. Flatten the top again if needed, then divide the upper surface into three using a scalpel. Bend the whole pistil slightly. Attach another piece of green paste at the base of the pistil to represent the ovary. Divide this into six.

4 Colour the pistil with a mixture of moss and primrose petal dust, making the ovary a little darker. The tip of the pistil is coloured with a touch of deep purple and aubergine. Dip into a ½ glaze, shake off excess, and leave to dry.

5 Tape the stamens around the pistil, making the pistil slightly higher than the stamens. Bend the stamens into the required position. (The more mature the flower is, the more curl the stamens should have.)

PETALS

6 Roll out some ivory flower paste, leaving a thick ridge down the centre. (You can use a grooved board or rolling pin if you wish.) Using lily cutters (or a scalpel and templates made from the outlines on page 140), cut out three large and three smaller petals. Insert a moistened 24-gauge wire into each petal, making sure that it is at least halfway up the ridge in the petal.

7 Vein the large petals in the larger veiner and the smaller petals in the smaller veiner, pressing the two sides of the veiners firmly to give a good impression. Place the petals on a pad and use the rounded end of the largest celstick to soften the edges, working half on the paste and half on the pad. The petals of some lilies have very frilled edges, but I prefer to give them only a little movement. Pinch down the centre of the whole length of each petal, especially strongly at the tips.

8 The three large petals have a hairy area towards the base. Using a pair of fine scissors, cut several fine hairs, holding the blades very close to the surface. Curl the hairs back using your finger. Curl the whole length of each petal and dry over a curved surface until firm enough to handle.

Colouring

9 Dust the base of each petal with primrose, and then over-dust half of this area with moss green. (The area to be coloured should be roughly the shape of a triangle.) The main colouring of the flower depends on your own personal taste as there are so many different variations. The petals illustrated are coloured using a mixture of plum, fuchsia and red. Dust the central area with this colour, then add a little depth using aubergine petal dust. Try to keep the colour away from the primrose at the base otherwise the results will be unattractive. The smaller petals tend to have less colour on them.

10 Using a fine paintbrush and a little cyclamen liquid colouring, paint on the spots; they should be stronger and slightly larger at the base. (It is always a good idea to have a photograph or the real flower to copy). Again, the smaller petals have fewer spots.

11 Dust the tip of each petal with the brush you used for the primrose and moss green. The colour should be very pale; cleaning your brush with a little cornflour will help to give a more subtle effect.

Assembly

12 Start by taping the larger petals around the base of the stamens using ½-width pale green tape. Add the smaller petals in between each of the larger ones, slightly recessed. If the petals are still slightly soft, you can now re-curl the petals if needed. Dust the back of the flower with a little moss green and primrose, making it darker towards the base.

Tape each flower on to an 18-gauge wire for strength.

Buds

13 Tape over an 18-gauge wire several times with ½-width green floristry tape. Bend a large hook in one end, and moisten the end. Roll a large sausage of paste and insert the wire into one end, making sure that it is firmly fixed. (I usually push the wire in at least halfway.)

14 To mark the impression of petals, make a 'cage' using three 24-gauge wires (see page 10). Open the cage and insert the bud, tip first. Arrange the wires equally and close them together so that they press into the paste and mark it equally into three. Release the cage and move each of the wires a few millimetres to one side. Close the cage again to form three ridges down the length of the bud. Remove the cage, and then, using your finger and thumb, pinch a deep ridge on the paste between each pair of division lines.

15 Dust the surface of the bud with a little of the flower colour, and over-dust with the primrose and moss green mixture. The base of the bud should be slightly darker so increase the moss green at the base. The smaller the buds are, the more green they should be.

16 Steam both the flowers and buds to give a waxy appearance (see page 10).

Leaves

17 Roll out some mid-holly/ivy paste using a grooved rolling pin or board. Cut out the leaves using a scalpel and templates made from the outlines on page 140. Insert a moistened 24-gauge wire into at least half of the length of the ridge on each leaf. Place each leaf on a pad and soften the edges using the rounded end of the largest cel-stick. Vein either by marking on some veins with a dresden tool, by veining with a double-sided veiner, or by using a fresh leaf. Allow to dry for about 1 hour.

18 Dust the leaves with dark green, and then over-dust with moss. The smaller leaves should be more of a lime green in colour. Dip each leaf into a ½ glaze, shake off excess, and leave to dry.

Chinese Jasmine

There are some 300 species of jasmine. *Jasminium polyanthum* is native to China, hence its common name. This plant is regularly used in bridal bouquets, its delicate white or pink-tinged flowers and slender foliage adding elegance to any spray.

Materials

White and mid-holly/ivy flower paste
24, 28 and 33-gauge wires
Fine stamens (optional)
Plum, moss, pink, dark green and holly/ivy petal dust (blossom tint)
¼ glaze (see page 10)

Equipment

Small stephanotis cutter (568)
Simple leaf cutters (229-232)
Pale green floristry tape

FLOWER

1 Form a small ball of white flower paste into a teardrop shape. Pinch out the broad end of the teardrop between your fingers and thumbs to form a pedestal. Place the shape down on a board and roll out the paste very finely using a small cel-stick. Place the stephanotis cutter over the thick part of the pedestal and cut out the flower. Rub your thumb over the cutter before removing the flower to make sure you have clean-cut edges to the petals.

2 Place the flower on a pad and, using the rounded end of the small celstick, soften the back of each petal, working half on the paste and half on the pad. Using the pointed end of the tool, open up the throat of the flower. Moisten the end of a 28-gauge wire and pull it through the centre of the flower, until the end is just hidden.

3 If you wish you can insert a fine stamen in the centre of the flower. Move the petals around a little to add some movement. The flower has such a very fine calyx that it is usually unnecessary to add one; if anything, mix a little moss and dark green petal dust and dust at the base of the flower.

BUDS

4 I tend to use many more buds than flowers, as they have a softer appearance and, more importantly, they are quicker to make! Form a tiny ball of white paste into a cone shape, and insert a dry 33-gauge wire into the broad end. (There is no need to use egg white with such a small piece.) Hold the base of the bud between your finger and thumb and gradually thin down the bud using a rubbing motion. Try to keep the tip of the bud very pointed.

LEAVES

5 The leaves can be cut freehand but I prefer to use cutters. I use simple leaf cutters, but before you use them for jasmine leaves you need to squeeze the sides inwards to make them very narrow. (I suggest that you buy a set for just this purpose.) Using a finely grooved board or rolling pin, roll out some mid-holly/ivy paste quite finely. Cut out the leaves using the prepared cutters. The leaves grow in groups of five, seven or nine, and the first leaf is always larger than the others.

6 Insert a moistened 33-gauge wire into the central ridge on each leaf, and then place them on a pad. Soften the edges with the rounded end of the small celstick. Draw down a central vein on each using the fine end of a dresden tool, and pinch down the centre of each leaf

with your finger and thumb. Allow to dry for about 30 minutes before dusting.

COLOURING AND ASSEMBLY

7 Group the buds and flowers into mixed clusters, taping them together with ¼-width green floristry tape.

8 Dust the upper surfaces of the buds with a touch of plum or pink petal dust. The flowers have even less colour on them, again only on the upper surface (it tends to be wherever the light catches them). Dust a little dark green and moss at the base of the buds.

9 Tape together the leaves using ¼-width tape again, starting with a large one and

then taping the others in pairs down the stem. Dust the upper surfaces heavily with dark green, and then over-dust with holly/ivy. Dip into a ¼ glaze, shake off excess, and leave to dry.

10 To form a climbing stem, tape over a 24-gauge wire with ½-width tape, and then tape the leaves on to it so that you have two groups coming out at the same point on either side of the stem. The flowers and buds always appear out of these leaf axils. Continue to build up the stem until it is the length you need.

Ivy

Ivy *(Hedera)* is probably one of the most useful forms of foliage, taking on many different shapes, colours and sizes. It is often used to symbolize fidelity, making it an ideal subject for a wedding cake! See pages 122–123 for instructions on how to make the Common Ivy.

Materials

Pale or mid-green flower paste
18, 24, 26 and 28-gauge wires
Holly/ivy, dark green, plum,
aubergine, blue, black and
white petal dust (blossom tint)
½ glaze (see page 10) or aerosol
confectioners' varnish
Clear alcohol (gin or vodka)

Equipment

Large ivy cutters
African ivy cutters
Pointed ivy cutters
Birdsfoot ivy, large ivy or large
nasturtium veiners (GI)
Pale green, beige and brown
floristry tape
Small piece of sponge

LEAVES

1 Roll out some green flower paste using a grooved rolling pin or board. The thickness of the paste will depend upon the size of leaf you are making – a larger leaf looks much better if it is slightly thicker. Cut out as many leaves as possible from one strip of paste, using your chosen shape of cutter. Cover the leaves that you are not working on with a sheet of plastic to stop them drying out too quickly.

2 Insert a suitable moistened wire into the central ridge on each leaf (the size of leaf determining the strength of wire required). Try to insert the wire into at least half the length of the leaf.

3 Vein all the leaves using double-sided veiners: the African and pointed ivy will both fit into the birdsfoot ivy veiners and either the large ivy or nasturtium veiner is ideal for the larger ivy leaves. (You can, if you wish, use the veiner as a template as well, simply cutting out the leaf shape using a scalpel or scissors.)

4 Soften the edges of the larger ivy leaves only as these tend to be thicker; softening the edges with a celstick helps to give a more realistic effect. For the smaller ivies, especially the pointed ivy, simply stretch the sections gently with your fingers. (If you soften these their shape becomes very distorted.) Allow to dry a little before taping over each stem with pale green floristry tape.

COLOURING

5 It is best to colour the leaves as soon as possible, as the dryer they are the more difficult it is to achieve dark effects. Dust first of all with holly/ivy on both sides of the leaf and add depth using dark green. Some ivies have plum or aubergine

Assembly

8 Tape over the end of a 24-gauge wire with ½-width beige or brown floristry tape. (Some varieties of ivy have darker stems than others.) Curl the end around a celstick to form a delicate start to the stem. (This part would usually be young leaves beginning to form.) It usually looks best in bouquets and arrangements if you start with smaller leaves and gradually work down to the larger ones. Work from one side of the stem to the other, adding leaves as singles or in pairs. For longer stems, it is advisable to strengthen the wire by adding an 18-gauge wire (or more for very long stems). When the required length has been achieved, bend the stem a little to give a more natural effect.

colouring to the edge of the leaf and this should be added at this stage. Allow to dry overnight and then either lay the leaves on greaseproof paper and spray with aerosol confectioners' varnish (which will give a high gloss) or dip into ½ glaze, shake off the excess, and allow to dry.

6 To create paler veins, support the leaf from behind with a finger, and use either a scalpel or a scriber to scratch off the colour and a little of the sugar until enough of the base colour is showing through. Start with the main veins, and then work on the finer ones to complete the leaf.

Variegated leaves

7 Mix together various greens with a touch of blue, black and white petal dust. Add some clear alcohol and, using a small piece of sponge, dab on some colour, adding darker green to areas of the leaf. Allow to dry, and glaze with ½ glaze. Pale veins can be scratched in if you wish (see step 6).

Eucharis Lily

Originating from South America, these unusual flowers (*Eucharis grandiflora*) are readily available throughout the year from any good florist's shop, being used mainly for bridal work. The word 'eucharis' is Greek for graceful or pleasing, which I think describes these flowers perfectly.

Materials

White and pale green flower paste
18, 24 and 28-gauge wires
Primrose, moss, spring green, champagne, nutkin and dark green petal dust (blossom tint)
Clear alcohol (gin or vodka)
Fine white stamens
½ glaze (see page 10)

Equipment

Eucharis lily cutters (670, 671)
White and pale green floristry tape
Amaryllis or other fine veiner

CORONA

1 Take a medium-sized ball of white flower paste and form it into a teardrop. Pinch out the paste at the broad end to form a mexican hat shape. Place the 'hat' on a board and thin out the brim using a celstick. Using the eucharis throat cutter, cut out the corona.

2 Hollow out the centre of the corona using the pointed end of a medium celstick, pressing the sides against the stick with your thumb. (The sides of the corona should be as straight as possible.) Press the rounded end of the celstick into the corona to create a flatter base.

3 Hook and moisten the end of a 24-gauge wire. Pull through the centre of the corona, embedding the hook deep into the base. Allow to dry.

4 The corona has six green lines radiating from the centre corresponding with each of the spikes on the edge. Mix a little moss and spring green petal dust with clear alcohol, and paint the markings on to the paste using a fine paintbrush. (These lines do not extend to the very ends of each point.) Dust a patch of spring green and primrose on either side of each line. (The more mature the flower, the paler the corona should be.)

STAMENS AND PISTIL

5 The stamens grow at the end of each spike on the corona. To make these, cut six short strands of stamen and attach one to the end of each spike to form 'T'-bars. Secure with a little softened flower paste. Allow to dry. Moisten the tips with egg white and dip into a mixture of champagne and nutkin petal dust.

6 The pistil is made by twisting a short piece of ¼-width white floristry tape to form a fine strand. Flatten the end using the broad end of a dresden tool; this will form a flap which needs to be cut into three with scissors. Place in the centre of the corona, using softened flower paste.

PETALS

7 Roll out some white flower paste using a grooved board or rolling pin. Cut out three petals using the single cutter, and insert a moistened 28-gauge wire into the central ridge of paste on each petal. Vein both sides of each petal.

8 Place the petals on a pad and soften the edges with a celstick. The edges are not very frilled so be careful not to overwork them. Taking each petal between your finger and

thumb, pinch a vein down the centre. Allow to dry slightly over the edge of the pad.

9 Repeat the above instructions to make three more petals for the outer layer. The base of each of these outer petals needs to be pinched from the upper surface to curl the edges back slightly.

10 Once all of the petals are firm enough to handle, tape the first three petals around the corona using ½-width floristry tape. The three outer petals are then taped in between the previous three.

11 The next part of this flower is optional, depending upon how the flowers are going to be displayed and whether the backs are going to show or not. The back of the eucharis lily is formed into a long, fine tube. To make this, add an extra piece of paste to the stem, blending it into the backs of the petals using the broad end of the dresden tool. Work the paste until it is smooth and the tube is the required length. Bend the flowers gently into shape.

12 Roll a ball of green paste to form the ovary and attach this to the base of the fine tube. Work the ovary between your finger and thumb until it is slightly oval in shape. Using a scalpel, divide the ovary into three and pinch each section down the centre to form a ridge.

13 Dust the ovary and the base of the tube using a mixture of moss and spring green petal dust. Glaze using a ½ glaze.

BUDS

14 Form a cone of white flower paste and insert a moistened 24-gauge wire into the base. Work the base of the cone between your finger and thumb until you have formed a fine tube. Using a scalpel, divide the top of the bud into three to give the impression of unopened petals. Add an ovary as for the flower.

ASSEMBLY

15 Tape together a collection of buds and flowers. (There are usually four or six flowers and buds to each stem.) To form a thicker stem, add an 18-gauge wire and pad out the stem using strips of kitchen paper taped over with ½-width green floristry tape.

16 There are two bracts at the base of the clump and these are cut out of green flower paste. Vein the bracts with a sweetcorn husk, soften the edges and mark a central vein on each with the fine end of the dresden tool. Moisten the base of the paste and attach to the flower stem. Dust with the green mixture and add a touch of primrose. Steam the flowers to give a waxy appearance (see page 10).

Stephanotis

Originating from Madagascar, this plant *(Stephanotis floribunda)* is often called Madagascan jasmine. It is a climbing plant with large dark green foliage and clusters of highly scented flowers that are always in great demand for bridal work.

FLOWER

1 Roll a ball of white flower paste into a sausage shape and pinch out one end to form a pedestal. Place the flat part of the pedestal on a board and roll out the paste using a small celstick, remembering that stephanotis produces a fairly thick, waxy flower. As the back of the flower is much wider than the centre of the nasturtium calyx cutter, it is easier to insert the back into one of the holes in a celpad, and to cut out the flower by pressing the cutter firmly against the soft pad.

2 Remove the flower and place the petals face down on the board. Using the small celstick again, broaden each petal, trying not to make the flower too fine. Each petal has an indent down the centre; to make this, place the flower back into the hole in the celpad and press the broad end of a dresden tool firmly on to each petal.

3 Open up the centre of the flower using the pointed end of a celstick, and insert a moistened 24-gauge wire. Holding the back of the flower directly behind the petals with your finger and thumb, work the paste to form a slender back that broadens towards the base. Trim off any excess paste. Dust the flower from the base with a mixture of spring green, moss and primrose. Add a small amount of this colour to the flower centre, along with a dash of champagne petal dust. Stephanotis can be either steamed (see page 10) or dipped in a ½ glaze to help give it its waxy appearance.

CALYX

4 Roll out some mid-green paste thinly and cut out the calyx using the small stephanotis cutter. The calyx does not have much shape

and I usually stick it straight on to the base of the flower. The calyx should be left flat; resist the temptation to stick the sepals on to the sides of the back of the flower.

BUD

5 Roll a ball of white paste into a cone shape. Hook and moisten a 24-gauge wire, and insert it into the base of the cone. Working the centre of the cone between your finger and thumb, elongate the bud to form its characteristic shape (it should be pointed at the top, narrow at the centre and broader towards the base which needs to be fairly flat).

6 Make a 'cage' (see page 10) with five 28-gauge wires. Insert the pointed end of the bud into the cage and close the cage over it to mark the impression of five unopened petals. Pinch each of the petals a little to make a ridge of paste between the wires before removing the cage.

7 Add a calyx as for the flower, using a smaller calyx cutter for the smaller buds. Dust with a mixture of spring green, moss and primrose from the base of each bud.

LEAVES

8 Roll out some mid-green paste using a grooved rolling board. Use a fresh leaf as a template and veiner, and cut around the edge with a scalpel. (For speed, you can use a set of large rose petal cutters and simply stretch each leaf after it has been cut.) Insert a suitable moistened wire into the central ridge in each leaf, making sure that you insert it to at least half the length of the leaf. Pinch down the centre and allow the leaves to dry fairly flat.

9 Dust the leaves heavily with dark green petal dust and

glaze using a ¾ glaze. Allow to dry and then remove the colour from the centre vein with a scalpel.

ASSEMBLY

10 Tape over the stems and tape flowers and buds into clusters of various sizes using ½-width pale green floristry tape. The main stem is an 18-gauge wire taped over with green tape. Add the smaller leaves in pairs, gradually working down to the larger ones. At any stage you can add the flower and bud clusters, starting usually with a cluster of buds, but every time you tape on a flower cluster you must add a pair of leaves at the same point. When you have made the required length, bend the whole stem to create an attractive display. Dust the stems with dark green petal dust.

Eustoma

This beautiful plant (*Lisianthus ressellianthus*) is a member of the Gentian family (it is often known as the prairie gentian). It gives a very delicate appearance to an arrangement, mainly due to its graceful twisted buds and fine stems.

Materials

White, pale melon and pale holly/ivy flower paste
20, 24, 26 and 33-gauge wires
Primrose, lemon, moss, deep purple, African violet, spring green, holly/ivy, white and dark green petal dust (blossom tint) ¼ glaze (page 10)

Equipment

Large rose petal cutters (550, 549)
Eustoma petal veiner (GI)
Ceramic silk veining tool (HP)
Fine pliers
Green floristry tape
Long-nosed tweezers
Cattleya orchid wing petal cutters (3, 6)

PETALS

1 Shape a ball of pale melon flower paste into a cone, and then roll it out thinly on a board, leaving a slightly raised area towards the pointed end. Cut out the petal using the chosen size of rose petal cutter.

2 Cut a length of 26-gauge wire into three. Moisten one end of a piece and insert it into the thick area of the petal. Because the flower is usually seen from the side, the wire is inserted only a little way into the base of the petal; a small hook can be made in the wire if you feel it needs some extra support. Pinch the base to make it slender.

3 Place the petal in a double-sided eustoma veiner, pressing firmly to give the full effect. Remove the petal and return it to the board.

4 Frill the upper edge of the petal with the ceramic veining tool or a cocktail stick (toothpick). Some flowers have more frills than others, so decide which you prefer. I find that quite a lot of frilling gives the flowers some movement.

5 Cup the centre of the petal gently using a large celstick. Make another four petals in exactly the same way. Allow to dry until firm enough to handle.

PISTIL

6 Cut a short length of 26-gauge wire, moisten the end and attach a small ball of pale holly/ivy paste to the end. Roll the paste between your finger and thumb until it covers a short piece of the wire very finely. Attach a larger piece of paste at the base, and form it into an oval shape to represent the ovary.

7 Roll a small sausage of paste and flatten both ends between your finger and thumb, so that it looks like a little bow-tie. Place the paste on a pad and hollow out both flattened ends using a small celstick. Pinch the centre slightly between your finger and thumb, giving the piece a heart-shaped appearance from the side.

8 Moisten the top of the wired pistil and position the heart shape on top, pressing firmly to make sure it is secure. In an immature flower this piece should be small and the two end sections squeezed closer together.

STAMENS

9 Cut five very short pieces of 33-gauge wire. Bend one end of each piece into a 'T'-bar shape. To do this, use pliers to bend the end at 90°, and then bend this small piece at the centre to form a 'T' shape. Attach a tiny sausage-shaped piece of white paste to the end (with pieces as small as this you won't need any egg white).

10 Tape the five stamens around the base of the pistil, so that their tops are a little higher than the ovary. Dust the tip of each stamen with primrose and lemon. Dust the top of the pistil with primrose and a touch of moss petal dust. Colour the ovary a dull green.

COLOURING AND ASSEMBLY

11 Dust the petals using your chosen colours. The petals illustrated are dusted with deep purple and African violet. The edge of each petal should be dark and the base very pale.

12 Tape the petals around the pistil and stamens, so that they overlap each other. You will need to tuck the last petal in underneath the first. While the petals are still damp, move them around and bend them into shape. Squeeze in the base of the petals to form the tight base characteristic of the flower. You might find that you have to stick the petals together using egg white, or a little flower paste softened with egg

white, as they have a tendency to move around. Hang the flower upside-down until it is a little dryer, and then curl back the edges of each petal. Tape on a 20-gauge wire for strength. Steam the flower (see page 10) to give a gentle sheen.

CALYX

13 The eustoma calyx is very fine. Roll five fine strands of pale holly/ivy flower paste. Attach them to the base of the flower with egg white. Allow to

the cage and twist the petals together from left to right.

16 Dust the bud with a little of the flower colour and a touch of pale spring green at the base. The smaller the bud, the less colour it should have. Add a calyx as for the flower.

LEAVES

17 Roll out some pale holly/ivy paste using a grooved rolling pin or board. (These leaves are quite fleshy.) Either cut the leaves freehand with a scalpel, or use orchid wing petal cutters. Insert a moistened 26-gauge wire into half the length of the leaf. Place on a pad and soften the edges with a celstick. Use the fine end of a dresden tool to draw down a central vein and a series of veins following the curved edge of each leaf.

18 Dust the leaves with a little dark green, and then over-dust with holly/ivy and white mixed together. Dip into a ¼ glaze, shake off excess, and leave to dry. Make as many leaves as you wish, remembering that they grow in pairs down the stem; each time you join buds or flowers together, there should be two leaves at the junction.

firm up, and then dust with a little dark green petal dust. (Alternatively, for general purposes, make the calyx from green floristry tape; this method avoids so many breakages!)

BUDS

14 Roll a ball of pale melon paste into a cone and insert a moistened 24-gauge wire. Work on the base of the cone to turn it into a more graceful shape.

15 To give the impression of petals, the easiest method is to make a 'cage' with five 26-gauge wires (see page 10). Place the bud, tip first, into the cage and close the wires around the bud as evenly as possible. While the wire is still in place, pinch out the paste from between the wires with your fingers or a pair of long-nosed tweezers. Release

Anemone

The anemone belongs to the *Ranunculaceae* family, which also includes buttercups. They are available from florists from November to May, making them an ideal choice for many occasions.

Materials

Pale melon, ivory and holly/ivy flower paste
20, 26 and 30-gauge wires
Violet, cornflower blue, plum, African violet, lavender, red, aubergine, dark green, spring green and moss petal dust (blossom tint)
Lace-making thread
Black pollen dust
¼ glaze (see page 10)

Equipment

Simple leaf cutters (228, 229, 230)
Round Christmas rose veiner (GI)
5mm (¼ in) flat-headed brush
Pale green floristry tape
Emery board
Daisy leaf cutter (J) or templates (see page 140)

PETALS

1 Roll out some pale melon paste thinly using a grooved rolling pin or board. Cut out the petals using the simple leaf cutters. Some anemones have more petals than others, and the size and shape can vary, even on one flower. I usually cut out 9–11 petals for each flower.

2 Cut lengths of white 30-gauge wire into four. Moisten the ends of the wires and insert one into the thick central ridge of each petal.

3 Vein each petal using a double-sided Christmas rose veiner, pressing firmly to give very definite veins. (Any other fine, fan-formation veiner could be used instead.)

4 Place the petals on a pad and frill the edges with a cocktail stick (toothpick) or with a celstick. Anemones vary so much that it is best to experiment to decide which you prefer. Cup the centre of each petal a little. Dry the petals for 15–30 minutes before you colour them; the strong colours are best achieved if the petals are dusted while they are still damp, as the petal dust adheres better.

COLOURING

5 Anemones are available in many different colours, ranging from strong, bold colours like purple, cerise and red, to paler, more delicate colours like mauve, pink and ivory. Some anemones are even bi-coloured. Using a 5mm (¼ in) flat-headed brush and your chosen colour, dust each petal with very firm strokes. The petals illustrated are coloured red, with a little aubergine on the edges. To achieve a very strong colour, steam each petal a little (see page 10), and then re-dust with your chosen colour. The backs of the petals should be slightly paler. Try to keep the base of each petal white, simply by avoiding this area when you dust. If you do dust over this

Note

The anemone has been cultivated since ancient times,
being native to the
Mediterranean countries and
parts of Asia. The red forms
would make a wonderful alternative to poinsettia in a
Christmas arrangement.

area, allow the petals to dry,
and then remove the colour
using a scalpel. (This actually
gives a slightly cleaner, more
realistic appearance.)

6 The purple flowers illustrated on page 31 are coloured
with a mixture of equal proportions of violet and cornflower
blue, and then over-dusted with
African violet. The paler flowers
are coloured with lavender and
a little of the violet mix. The
cerise flowers are dusted with
plum, with a little aubergine on
the edges. The ivory flowers can
be left plain or given a plum or
red tinge at the base.

STAMENS

7 Most anemone centres are
blackish-blue, although there
are some ivory forms that have
creamy-green stamens. The filaments of each stamen tend to be
the same colour as the flower.

8 Bend a length of 30-gauge
wire in half. Hold the bend
in the wire between your finger
and thumb, and twist it to form
a small loop. Set aside.

9 Wrap some fine white thread
around two parted fingers
many times. Remove from your
fingers and twist this large loop
into a figure-of-eight shape.
Bend this in half to form a
smaller loop.

10 Place the prepared wire
through the centre and
tape over the base of the thread
with floristry tape, down on to
the wire. (The small loop of wire
should still be visible in the centre of the thread.) You might
have enough thread for two sets
of stamens; if this is the case,
prepare another piece of wire as
before and place it through the
other side of the loop. Tape
over, and then cut the thread in
half. Trim the stamens a little,
trying to cut the thread into a
gentle curve.

11 Rub the tips of the stamens against an emery
board to give them a little more
bulk. Dust the thread with the
colour of the flower.

12 The centre of a real
anemone can be very
large; it is more attractive if kept

fairly small. Roll a ball of paste
and flatten the base. Place the
ball on a cocktail stick (toothpick), and use a pair of fine scissors to texture the surface. Paint
the surface with egg white and
dip it into some black pollen
dust mixed with violet and
cornflower blue petal dust.

13 Place the centre on the
hook in the middle of the
stamens. To add pollen to the
stamen tips, paint a little egg
white on your board, rub the
tips of the thread gently in the
egg white, and then quickly dip
the tips into the black pollen
mixture. Be very careful – if you
dip them in too far you will end
up with a very ugly centre; too
little and it will look patchy.
Allow to dry.

ASSEMBLY

14 Tape the stamens on to a
piece of 20-gauge wire
using ½-width tape. If you have
made any small petals, these
should be taped on first. I usually tape a few petals on at a
time, adding them opposite
each other. Gradually add the

larger petals, until you feel that the flower looks finished. Some flowers will look better with more petals than others.

15 Tape over the main stem several times with ½-width tape to create the characteristic fleshy stem.

BUD

16 Tape over a piece of 20-gauge wire and bend a large hook in the end. Attach a medium-sized ball of paste to the end. Allow to dry.

17 Roll out some ivory flower paste thinly, and cut out five or six petals using one of the simple leaf cutters. Vein both sides of each petal using the Christmas rose veiner. Frill or soften the edges of each petal and stick on to the prepared dried centre. Position the petals in a very informal way (if you make them too neat the bud will look like a badly made rose!). Flatten the tops of the petals to give a tighter appearance.

18 Dust the bud while the paste is still damp. Steam (see page 10), and dust again.

LEAVES

19 Anemones do not have a calyx, but they have a very interesting leaf formation behind each flower. Roll out some mid-holly/ivy paste fairly thickly using a grooved board or rolling pin. Cut out the leaves using the daisy leaf cutter, or use a scalpel and templates made from the outlines on page 140. Trim away the bottom piece of each shape, leaving three sections per leaf.

20 Insert a moistened 26-gauge wire into the central ridge of paste, so that it runs almost to the tip of the leaf. This leaf is very fragile and needs a lot of support. Broaden each of the sections by rolling them with a celstick. Using a scalpel, cut out some 'V' shapes from the edge of each leaf to give a 'frillier' effect. Flatten and thin the edges using the broad end of a dresden tool. Vein the leaf using the fine end of the tool (or use a fresh leaf). You will need a mixture of sizes.

21 Dust each leaf with some dark green petal dust, and give the edges a tinge of plum. Over-dust with either moss green or spring green (the depth can vary from stem to stem). Dip into a ¼ glaze, shake off excess and leave to dry.

22 Tape three or four leaves behind each bud and flower. The more mature the flower is, the further down the stem the leaves should be, but the leaves are taped tightly behind each bud.

Eucalyptus

Eucalyptus is a very versatile foliage, which can create a lovely soft feel with its silver-blue-green colouring. There are many types of eucalyptus; my favourite is this very large-leafed form. Another type has leaves with bronze-red edges, which are ideal for autumn arrangements.

Materials
Very pale holly/ivy flower paste
20, 26 and 28-gauge wires
Dark green, holly/ivy, white, aubergine and black petal dust (blossom tint)
¼ glaze (see page 10)

Equipment
Circle or rose petal cutters
Fine rose leaf veiner
Fresh eucalyptus leaves (optional)
Pale green floristry tape

LEAVES

1 Roll some flower paste out using a grooved rolling pin or board, remembering that the finished leaves should be slightly 'fleshy'. Cut out the leaves using the circle cutters, or use a scalpel and a fresh leaf as a template.

2 Cut a length of 26-gauge or 28-gauge wire into five. Moisten one end of a piece of wire and insert it into the thick central ridge of a leaf. The wire should be inserted into at least half the length of the leaf.

Repeat with more wires and leaves. Elongate each leaf by stretching the paste with your fingers.

3 Place the leaves on a pad and soften the edges with a celstick, just enough to remove the cut edges. Vein the leaf using either a fresh leaf or a very fine rose leaf veiner. These leaves tend to be very flat, but I do dry some of them on a gentle curve. You will need to make a variety of sizes for each stem, remembering that the leaves grow in pairs down the stem.

COLOURING

4 Start colouring the leaf using a flat-headed brush and a little dark green petal dust to add depth to the leaf. Over-dust gently with holly/ivy and a little white. Dust the edges and the base of each leaf with aubergine petal dust. Dip into a ¼ glaze, shake off excess, and allow to dry. As these leaves have a very dusty look their

appearance is improved if you over-dust with white petal dust (be very generous with this colour). Add a little black colour to parts of the leaf for more depth, if required. (One of the lustre colours can be used at this stage if you want to create a very soft effect.)

ASSEMBLY

5 At the top of each stem there are a few fine stems. The florist usually cuts these off, but, if time allows, I use them. They can be made from pieces of ¼-width tape, each twisted back on itself to make a fine strand.

6 Start to tape the stem up by taping two or three fine

stems on to the end of a 20-gauge wire using ½-width tape. Start by adding the small leaves in pairs and, as you work down the stem, add the medium and then the larger leaves. If you are making a very long stem, you might find that you will need an extra 20-gauge wire for strength and to give the appearance of more bulk. Smaller stems can be taped on to longer ones to give variation.

7 Dust the main stem with a little dark green and a lot of aubergine petal dust. At this final stage you might find you have to dust some more white or aubergine on to the leaves. Bend the main stem and the leaves to add movement to the whole piece.

Ladder Fern

There are many cultivated forms of this attractively bold plant (*Nephrolepsis*). They are quite simple to make and, because of their size, you don't need many to fill in the gaps in a bouquet. This fern is, however, very fragile and it is advisable to wire them into the bouquet before they are fully dried.

FERN FROND

1 Roll out a large piece of green paste not too thinly. Cut out the shape using the sword fern cutter. (You might find that it is easier to place the paste on top of the cutter and then roll your rolling pin over the top to obtain a cleaner cut.)

2 Remove the paste from the cutter and place the shape on the board. Frill both edges of each 'leaf' using the broad end of a dresden tool. Place the frond on a pad and draw a central vein on each of the 'leaves' using the fine end of the dresden tool.

3 Tape over a length of 24-gauge wire with ¼-width pale green floristry tape. Paint egg white on to the wire, covering a length the same as the length of the fern. Place the moistened wire down the centre of the fern. Press the wire firmly on to the paste to make sure that it is secure. Quickly turn the fern over. You should now have a ridge on the back of the leaf. Pinch either side of this ridge from the tip to the base using a pair of tweezers (to make the wire more secure). Turn the fern back over and pinch the tip of each section. Curl them in the required direction before you allow them to dry a little.

COLOURING

4 Dust the fern to various depths; the younger the fern is the lighter it should be. Start by dusting with dark green, then moss, and then over-dust with vine green. Dip into a ¼ glaze, shake off the excess, and leave to dry.

Materials

Mid-green flower paste
24-gauge wires
Vine green, moss and dark
green petal dust (blossom tint)
¼ glaze (see page 10)

Equipment

Sword fern cutter (J)
Pale green floristry tape
Tweezers

Fern

Although this fern has features of many different species, it is purely the work of my imagination! I always feel it is important to create interesting foliage; it doesn't always have to be exactly correct. This fern is easier to wire into a bouquet because each section is wired separately.

Materials
Pale green flower paste
20, 24, 30 and 33-gauge wires
Moss, dark green, skintone,
white (optional) and mother
of pearl (optional) petal dust
(blossom tint)
¼ glaze (see page 10)

Equipment
Australian fern cutters (three sizes)
Pale green floristry tape

'LEAVES'

1 Roll out the paste on a finely grooved board. (You will need to roll the paste very finely for this small fern.) Cut out the fern sections in various sizes, remembering that they grow in pairs down the stem. Insert a 33-gauge or 30-gauge wire, depending on the size of the piece.

2 Work on the edges of the pieces, using the broad end of a dresden tool to create a feathered effect. Mark a central vein on each piece with the fine end of the tool, then pinch down the centre of each piece and curve slightly if you wish.

COLOURING

3 Dust each piece with moss and dark green, with a little skintone on the edges. The backs can be dusted with mother of pearl if you wish. Glaze using a ¼ glaze. For a winter display, these ferns also look very good dusted all over with white petal dust to give a frosted appearance.

4 Tape a small piece of fern on the end of a 24-gauge wire to form the start of the frond, and then add some more small 'leaves' in pairs just below this. When you feel that the frond needs to be wider, start adding the medium and then the large 'leaves'. If you are making a very long piece of fern, you will need to add 20-gauge wire to support the weight. Bend the main stem into the desired shape and then dust with the green petal dusts.

Clivia

There are only four species of Clivia and they are all native to South Africa. They are mainly orange although there is a rare yellow form. The flower that I have copied *(Clivia gardenii)* is a variety that can be bought as a pot plant.

Materials

26 and 28-gauge wires
White, pale melon and mid-holly/ivy flower paste
Lemon, primrose, tangerine, red, coral and moss green petal dust (blossom tint)
¼ and ½ glazes (see page 10)

Equipment

Fine pliers
White and green floristry tape
Clivia petal cutters (610, 611)
Very large alstroemeria veiner (GI)

STAMENS AND PISTIL

1 Cut six short lengths of 28-gauge wire. Bend a closed hook in one end of each wire using pliers. Hold the hook at its centre and bend it into a 'T'-bar shape. Tape over the straight length of each wire with ¼ -width white floristry tape.

2 Attach a tiny sausage of white paste to each 'T'-bar. (I usually find that I do not need any egg white for such a small piece.) Moisten the surface of the paste and dip it into lemon petal dust to form the pollen. Dust the length of the wire with a pale mixture of moss and primrose petal dust.

3 To form the pistil, tape over another piece of 28-gauge wire with white tape, leaving a flap of tape at the top. Cut this flap into three, using a scalpel or fine scissors, and then twist each piece between your finger and thumb to form three fine strands. Dust with the pale green mixture as for the stamens.

PETALS

4 Roll out some pale melon paste using a grooved board or rolling pin, and cut out three petals using the large clivia petal cutter.

5 Insert a moistened 26-gauge wire into the central ridge of each petal. Vein each of the petals using the double-sided alstroemeria veiner, then place on a pad and soften the edges a little with a celstick. Clivia have quite a stiff appearance so do not try to frill the paste. Pinch a ridge down the centre of each petal from the base to the tip, and allow to firm a little over a gentle curve.

6 Cut out three more petals with the smaller cutter, and repeat step 5.

COLOURING AND ASSEMBLY

7 Dust a patch of lemon and primrose from the base of each petal, tapering to a slight point approximately halfway up. Colour the remainder of each petal with tangerine and coral, and then over-dust with a little red. Dip each petal into a ¼

glaze, shake off excess, and
leave to dry.

8 Tape the stamens together
around the pistil, which
should be slightly taller. Bend
the stamens into shape, with the
anthers curving inwards.

9 Tape the three large petals
around the stamens, and
then tape the smaller ones in
between using ½-width green
floristry tape. As the paste is
still soft, bend each petal back a
little at the tip.

OVARY

10 Attach a ball of green
paste at the base of the
petals. Mark it into three using a
scalpel, and then pinch each section down the centre between
your finger and thumb to form
a ridge. Dust with moss green
and glaze using a ½ glaze.

BUD

11 Form a cone of paste and
insert a 26-gauge or 28-
gauge wire, depending on the
size of the bud. Work the base
of the cone between your finger
and thumb to form a more slender shape. Divide the bud into
three using a 'cage' made from
three 26-gauge wires (see page
10). Insert the bud, tip first, into
the cage and close the wires
over it, keeping them as evenly

spaced as possible. Open the
cage and remove the bud. Pinch
a ridge with your finger and
thumb down the centre of each
section now marked on the bud.
Add an ovary as before. Dust
with the same colours as the
flower, then dip in ¼ glaze,
shake off the excess, and leave
to dry.

12 Tape the flowers and
buds together. They all
appear from the same point. At
the base of the flower head
there are some bracts which can
be made with either tape or
paste. The stems are flat on both
sides. I usually use the flowers
as single pieces rather than in a
full flower head.

Oncidium Orchid

This is one of the larger hybrids of Oncidium orchid, although it is still a comparatively small flower, making it an ideal filler to use in an arrangement with larger flowers. I prefer the yellow varieties, but there are many other colours to choose from.

Materials
Pale melon flower paste
20, 24, 26 and 28-gauge wires
Lemon, primrose, red, skin-tone and nutkin petal dust (blossom tint)
Clear alcohol (gin or vodka)

Equipment
Oncidium orchid throat cutter (656)
Ceramic silk veining tool (HP)
Nasturtium petal cutter (446)
Medium stephanotis cutter (566)
Pale green floristry tape

THROAT PETAL

1 Roll out some pale melon flower paste using a grooved rolling pin or board. Cut out the petal using the oncidium throat cutter. Insert a moistened 26-gauge wire into the whole length of the central ridge of paste.

2 Using the ceramic silk veining tool, frill the edges of the petal, leaving the two tiny pieces unfrilled. If you want the edge to be a little more jagged, use the broad end of a dresden tool to double frill the edge (see page 8).

3 Soften and cup the two tiny pieces of the petal, and then pinch down the length of the

whole petal to form a centra vein.

4 For smaller flowers, use the nasturtium petal cutter instead. Cut out a curved 'V' shape at the base and add two small pieces of paste at the top of the petal, where the paste joins the wire. Then work on the petal exactly as before.

OUTER PETALS

5 Roll out some more pale melon paste, leaving a raised area in the centre. (You could use a mexican hat board (see page 8) to achieve this.) Cut out the petal shape using the stephanotis cutter, making sure that the thick area of the paste is in the centre of the cutter. Before you remove the paste from the cutter, rub your thumb on the paste around the edge of the cutter to make sure you have cleanly cut edges.

6 Imagine the shape as a person, and then frill the edges of the two 'arms' using the broad end of a dresden tool. Place the piece on a pad and

often the other three petals using a bone-end tool. Cup the 'head' petal forward, turn the shape over and curl the 'legs' back.

7 Moisten the centre of the paste and pull through the throat petal so it fits securely. Curl the 'head' petal forwards again, if necessary, and the others slightly back.

8 Roll a tiny ball of paste into a teardrop shape and attach it to the top of the throat petal, between the two smaller sections. Blend into the surface using the broad end of the dresden tool. (This forms the column.) On a real flower, there is a raised piece on the petal below the column, but I prefer to leave this off as it can give a slightly ugly appearance. Allow to dry a little before colouring.

BUDS

9 Attach cone-shaped pieces of paste to 28-gauge wires. Divide the surface of each bud into five using a 'cage' made from five 28-gauge wires (see

Page 10). Make lots of buds of various sizes.

COLOURING AND ASSEMBLY

10 Dust the throat and the back petals with a mixture of primrose and lemon petal dust. Paint the back petals in very untidy stripes using nutkin and skintone petal dust mixed with a little alcohol. Paint some markings on the throat using red and skintone, forming a combination of stripes and spots.

11 Dust the buds with the yellow mixture, and then paint on horizontal stripes using the nutkin brown mixture.

12 Tape together a small group of buds and flowers on to a 24-gauge wire, alternating from one side of the stem to the other. Tape these small groups on to a 20-gauge wire to form a larger stem.

Winter Wedding Cake

Although the flowers on this wedding cake are available all year round, together they create a wintry feel. I'm very fond of combining white flowers with strong green foliage; here the two together make a very bold yet elegant design.

Materials

15cm (6 in), 23cm (9 in) and 30cm (12 in) round cakes
Apricot glaze
3kg (6lb) almond paste (marzipan)
Clear alcohol (kirsch or vodka)
5kg (10lb) white sugarpaste
Fine willow green ribbon to trim cakes
Green velvet ribbon to trim boards and stand
18-gauge wires

Equipment

23cm (9 in), 30cm (12 in) and 43cm (17 in) round cake boards
Sugarpaste smoothers
'E'-shaped chrome stand (CV)
Double-sided sticky tape
Beige floristry tape
Florists' staysoft
Small shallow plastic container

Flowers

6–7 ivy stems, various lengths (see page 22)
3–4 eucharis lilies (see page 24)
3–4 creamy-white half roses and 4–5 buds (see page 14)
2 full stems of stephanotis (see page 26)
5 caladium leaves, various sizes (see page 63)
Winter Wedding Arrangement (see page 45)

PREPARATION

1 Brush the cakes with apricot glaze and cover with almond paste. Leave to dry overnight. Brush the cakes with alcohol, and cover the cakes and boards separately with white sugarpaste, using sugarpaste smoothers to achieve a good finish. Position the cakes on the cake boards and allow to dry. Fasten fine willow green ribbon around the base of each cake, and velvet ribbon around the board edges.

2 Cover the long upright piece of the cake stand with green velvet ribbon, using a little double-sided sticky tape at the beginning and end. Place the cakes on the stand, positioning the upright piece of the stand to the left of the cakes.

FLORAL ARRANGEMENTS

3 Arrange some long stems of ivy on the middle tier to cover the top edge and right-hand side of the cake. You will need to add some extra 18-gauge wires to strengthen the stems, taping the whole piece together with full-width beige floristry tape. Curve the stems to follow the line of the cake, and simply place them on the cake's surface.

4 Follow the instructions on page 45 to make the large Winter Wedding Arrangement

that is displayed to the left of the cake. The base of the arrangement should sit on the cake board of the bottom tier, and the tallest piece of ivy should curl in front of the middle tier.

5 To make the smaller cake top arrangement, use the flowers and foliage listed above, arranging them in florists' staysoft in a small, shallow plastic container.

Note

As well as using smoothers, a good way to achieve a silky smooth finish on sugarpaste is to flatten a ball of sugarpaste in the palm of your hand and to smooth it over the paste. This is especially good for smoothing the top edges of cakes.

Winter Wedding Arrangement

This arrangement is quite an unusual shape, but it fits very well with the design of the cake on page 42. It could also be used with a single or two-tiered cake, with the top part of the arrangement curving over the cake.

Flowers

7–9 ivy stems, various lengths (see page 22)
3 trailing stephanotis stems, plus one small piece (see page 26)
10–11 eucharis lilies (see page 24)
7 caladium leaves, various sizes (see page 63)
11–12 creamy white roses with foliage (see page 14)

Equipment

18-gauge wires
Pale green floristry tape
Pliers
Wire cutters
Florists' staysoft
Small shallow plastic container

1 As this is a large arrange-ment you will need to strengthen the stems of the taller flowers and foliage with 18-gauge wires, taping over using ½-width floristry tape.

2 Place a large clump of staysoft in a shallow plastic container. Start by arranging the ivy foliage, shaping it to look like a large ornate 'L' shape. Push in the stephanotis stems, positioning them alongside some of the ivy stems.

3 The eucharis lilies are the main flowers of the design, so place these in next. Push most of the stems in vertically and a few horizontally. The larger flowers should be placed at the centre of the arrangement to form the focal point. Fill in behind the eucharis lilies with the caladium leaves. (These will help add depth and detail at the same time with their interesting veining.)

4 Finally, tape up some of the roses into twos and threes, and push these in to fill in the gaps around the focal point, and to follow the lines of the ivy on the outer edges of the arrange-ment.

5 When you have everything in place, stand back and take a look at the arrangement from a distance. Sometimes you can spot mistakes that you are unable to see close up. If there are gaps or the whole shape needs defining, add some more foliage.

Mothering Sunday Cake

The glass plate on which this cake is displayed is hand-painted, making it the perfect gift. Once the cake has been eaten, both the anemone spray and the plate can be kept as reminders of the day!

Materials

20cm (8 in) round cake
Apricot glaze
750g (1½ lb) almond paste
(marzipan)
Clear alcohol (kirsch or vodka)
750g (1½ lb) champagne sugarpaste
Fine pink and purple ribbon to trim cake

Equipment

Sugarpaste smoothers
38cm (15 in) perspex or glass plate
Selection of paintbrushes
Magenta, red, violet, black, light green, dark green, yellow and white glass paints
Posy pick
Green floristry tape

Flowers

5 anemones, assorted colours (see page 31)
5 anemone buds (see page 33)
5 rose buds and 4 half roses (see page 14)
5 fronds of ladder fern (see page 36)
35 large ivy leaves (see page 22)

PREPARATION

1 Brush the cake with apricot glaze and cover with almond paste. Leave to dry overnight. Moisten the almond paste with clear alcohol, and cover the cake with sugarpaste, using sugarpaste smoothers to achieve a good finish. Allow to dry.

GLASS PAINTING

2 This technique is very attractive when used to decorate base boards, perspex pillars, dividers and cake stands. The design will be permanent once it has been allowed to dry thoroughly. Before you carry out any work, make sure that the

piece you are going to work on is clean and dry. The design was painted on to the plate free-hand, but if you need guidance the pattern on page 140 should help you get started. You don't necessarily need to be neat or accurate with your design, as long as the colours are clean and balanced.

3 Using a broad, flat paintbrush, paint the flower petals on to the glass, cleaning the brush each time you change colours. (I used the colours neat, occasionally mixing them together to form slightly different tones.) Next, paint the leaves into the design using green and yellow colours, outlining here and there with a little magenta.

4 Once the flowers are dry, you can paint in the black anemone centres, this time using a smaller brush. Start by

painting in the large round centre, then surround it with small dots to represent the stamens.

5 Outline areas of the design with diluted black paint, if needed. Allow the entire design to dry thoroughly.

ASSEMBLY

6 Position the cake on the painted glass plate. Attach a band of fine purple ribbon around the base of the cake and a pink ribbon slightly above it. Tie two small bows of ribbon, one of each colour, and position over the joins. Push a posy pick into the top of the cake.

7 Arrange the flowers and foliage in a suitably shaped spray, taping the wires together with floristry tape, and creating a handle. Insert the handle into the posy pick, and arrange the flowers as necessary.

Golden Days

This cake was designed to celebrate a golden wedding anniversary, but would be equally suitable as a 50th birthday cake. The large arrangement includes a variety of flowers from various parts of the world; together they create an autumnal feel, mainly due to the varied colours of the virginia creeper and cotinus foliage.

Materials

3kg (6lb) sugarpaste
Gold and dark green spray paints (optional)
30cm (12 in) teardrop cake
Apricot glaze
1.5kg (3lb) almond paste (marzipan)
Autumn leaf paste colouring
Clear alcohol (kirsch or vodka)
Fine brown ribbon to trim cake
Green ribbon to trim boards
Pale green flower paste
Moss, dark green, holly/ivy, aubergine, red, tangerine and white petal dust (blossom tint)
½ glaze (see page 10)
Royal icing

Equipment

43cm (17 in) round cake board
36cm (14 in) teardrop cake board
Virginia creeper templates (see page 143)
Hydrangea leaf veiners (GI)
Tilting cake stand

Flowers

Golden Days Arrangement (see page 51)

PREPARATION

1 Cover the large round cake board with sugarpaste and allow to dry for at least 1 week as this will form the base for the whole piece. Colour the sugarpaste on the board with dark green spray paint, or if you prefer to use food colouring, paint with dark green and holly/ivy petal dust mixed together and diluted with clear alcohol. Overspray the green with a fine haze of gold. (When using spray paint, always work in a well-ventilated area.)

2 Brush the cake with apricot glaze and cover with almond paste. Leave to dry overnight. Colour 2kg (4lb) sugarpaste with autumn leaf paste colouring. Moisten the cake with alcohol, and cover the cake and teardrop board separately with sugarpaste. Transfer the cake on to the board, making sure you have a neat join between the cake and the board. Attach fine brown ribbon around the base of the cake and broader green ribbon around the board edge.

DECORATION

3 Roll out some pale green flower paste and use the virginia creeper templates (see page 143) to cut out some leaves with a scalpel. (You will need a good variation in size.) Vein each leaf using the hydrangea veiners, and then soften the edges with a large celstick. Pinch each leaf down the centre and allow to dry for 10–15 minutes.

4 Place the leaves on absorbent kitchen paper and dust with a variety of petal dusts, starting with the greens, and then adding red and aubergine to darken. Dip each leaf into a ½ glaze, shake off the excess, and allow to dry. Attach the leaves to the cake using a small amount of royal icing.

5 Paint some leaf stems and a main stem on to the cake to correspond with the paste leaves, using a mixture of dark green and holly/ivy petal dust diluted with a little clear alcohol. To create the paler veins on each leaf, use a fine paintbrush and some white and pale green petal dust mixed with a little alcohol, starting with the central vein and then painting in the finer veins.

6 To make the design easier on the eye, dust around the leaves with tangerine and holly/ivy. Dust the left-hand edge of the cake with a little tangerine petal dust, carrying the colour down on to the cake board. Add this colour very gently at first.

7 Place the cake on the display board using a tilting cake stand to prop the cake up at an angle. Position the flower arrangement in the gap created by the curve on the left-hand side of the cake.

Golden Days Arrangement

Once the cake has been cut and the party is over, you can use this arrangement as a room decoration, and as a memento of a happy celebration.

Flowers

5 stems of Chinese virginia creeper (see page 92)
7 stems of clivia (see page 38)
5 large stems of oncidium orchid (see page 40)
Several pieces of cotinus foliage (see page 101)
7 stems of montbretia (see page 94)

Equipment

30cm (12 in) bronze candle-stick
Gold spray paint
Glue gun and glue sticks
Florists' staysoft or oasis
18-gauge wires
Pale green floristry tape
Fine pliers
Wire cutters

PREPARATION

1 Spray the candlestick lightly with gold spray paint, leaving some of the base colour showing through. Allow to dry thoroughly.

2 Using the glue gun, stick a large ball of florists' staysoft to the candlestick. (If you prefer, dry oasis can be used instead.)

3 The long stems and heavier flowers will need extra support, so tape an extra 18-gauge wire to the main stem of each one. (The long stems of clivia will need two 18-gauge wires.)

4 Start by inserting the virginia creeper stems into the staysoft to form the outline of the arrangement. Add the pieces of clivia, positioning one clump as the focal point and spacing the others apart, working from one side of the arrangement to the other.

5 Add the oncidium orchids in the gaps between the virginia creeper and fill in the area around the focal point with the cotinus foliage. (This also adds a lot of depth to the arrangement.)

6 To complete the arrangement, thread in the montbretia stems, spacing the colour throughout. When you have finished, take a look at the arrangement from a distance, and then fill in any gaps with extra foliage, or correct errors that are not always obvious close up.

Floral Elegance

This spectacular two-tiered cake was made to celebrate my parents' pearl wedding anniversary. The design could also be used to great effect as a wedding cake, with the ever-popular combination of lilies and roses.

Materials

20cm (8 in) and 30cm (12 in) elliptical cakes
Apricot glaze
2kg (4lb) almond paste (marzipan)
Clear alcohol (kirsch or vodka)
3kg (6lb) white sugarpaste
Royal icing
Fine magenta ('beauty') ribbon

Equipment

Sugarpaste smoothers
25cm (10 in) and 40cm (16 in) elliptical cake boards
Plain scalloped crimpers
No. 1 piping tube (tip)
Double tilting cake stand
Double-sided carpet tape
50cm (20 in) silver candlestick

Flowers

Floral Elegance Curved Bouquet (see page 55)
Small Floral Elegance Spray

PREPARATION

1 Brush both of the cakes with apricot glaze and cover with almond paste. Allow to dry overnight. Moisten the cakes with clear alcohol, and cover with white sugarpaste, using sugarpaste smoothers to achieve a good finish. Cover the cake boards with sugarpaste and crimp the edges using a pair of plain scalloped crimpers.

Transfer the cakes to the boards, making sure you have neat joins between the cakes and boards. Pipe a snail's trail border around the base of each cake with royal icing and a no. 1 piping tube. Allow the piping to dry overnight, then attach a band of ribbon and a small bow at the base of each cake.

2 Make the curved bouquet as described on page 55. The small bouquet is simply a smaller version of the large one.

ASSEMBLY

3 Position both cakes on the tilting cake stand, using double-sided carpet tape to hold them in place. Tie the large bouquet on to the candlestick with some fine ribbon. Position the candlestick behind the cake, trailing the long ivy stem on to the lower cake's surface. The smaller spray is positioned next to the base tier, again trailing some of the foliage on to the cake and board so that the whole cake is framed.

Floral Elegance Curved Bouquet

This style of bouquet is very popular with brides, and is a useful shape to use on cakes, although it does not have to be made on the same scale as the one pictured opposite.

Flowers

1 long stem and 4 shorter stems of large ivy (see page 22)
4–5 stems of eustoma (see page 28)
3 stargazer lilies (see page 17)
3 dark pink roses (see page 14)
6 dark pink rose buds with foliage (see page 14)
5 stems of eucalyptus (see page 34)

Equipment

18-gauge wires
Pale green floristry tape
Fine pliers
Wire cutters

PREPARATION

1 First of all, strengthen any of the flower stems that are to be very long or that are particularly heavy, by taping in additional 18-gauge wires.

ASSEMBLY

2 Decide how long you want the bouquet to be. The first long stem of ivy needs to measure approximately two thirds the length of the whole bouquet. Bend the stem to a 90° angle. Add the other ivy stems, bending each to the same angle and taping each piece in with ½-width floristry tape. (The aim is to form a handle to the bouquet.) Together the ivy stems should form the basic outline of the bouquet. This type of bouquet should be heavier towards one side, so you will need to use longer and more stems of foliage on the heavier side. If the shape is created symmetrically, you will form a 'shower' bouquet instead.

3 Start to tape in the eustoma flowers, then tape the lilies into the bouquet, following a diagonal line. Choose one lily for the focal point and position it a little higher than the others. Add any extra eustoma flowers and buds to fill in the gaps.

4 Tape in the roses, using the larger ones in the middle of the bouquet and the buds towards the edges, curving the stems to follow the lines of the ivy stems. Finally, fill in the remaining gaps using the eucalyptus and any other foliage. Neaten the handle of the bouquet using full-width tape.

5 To display a bouquet of this size on a cake you would need to use a Wilton-crystal-effect plastic pillar, as the normal size of posy pick is too small. For the cake on page 52, the flowers are displayed off the cake, tied to a large candlestick with a length of ribbon.

Exotic Flowers

EXOTIC FLOWERS make a very bold, colourful and unusual decoration for a cake. Although most originated in tropical and subtropical areas of the world, many have for so long been successfully grown locally or imported that they can hardly be considered 'exotic'. They can be used in numerous combinations to create new and interesting arrangements which automatically have a very modern and exciting appearance.

Bauhinia

This plant *(Bauhinia variegata)* originates from India, and is sometimes called 'camel's foot' because of the shape of its leaf! This large genus is very diverse in shape, size, colour and form. The first flowers appear before the leaves; it is only at the end of the flowering season that the two can be seen together.

Materials

24, 26 and 28-gauge wires
Cream, pink, deep purple, plum, fuchsia, aubergine, dark green, primrose, moss and holly/ivy petal dust (blossom tint)
White, pale pink, pale green and mid-green flower paste
Cyclamen liquid food colouring
½ glaze (see page 10)

Equipment

Fine pliers
Pale green floristry tape
Bauhinia cutters (460–462)
Amaryllis veiner (or similar)
Black bryony veiner (GI)

STAMENS

1 Cut five pieces of 28-gauge wire. Holding the end of a wire with pliers, bend approximately 5mm (¼ in) down close to the main section, then bend from the centre of this piece to form a 'T'-bar. Colour each wire with plum petal dust.

2 Attach a tiny sausage-shaped piece of white flower paste to each 'T'-bar (this forms the anther), paint with egg white and then dip into cream petal dust to form the pollen. Allow to dry. Bend each stamen into an 'S' shape, using the pliers and pinching at intervals to create a gentle curve.

PISTIL

3 Roll a pea-sized ball of mid-green paste. Moisten the end of a 24-gauge wire, and thread the ball on to it. Holding the

paste firmly between your finger and thumb, work the paste down the wire to cover approximately 5cm (2 in) of the wire. Tape the stamens around the pistil, positioning them so that the tip of the pistil is slightly above the stamens.

PETALS

4 Roll out some pale pink paste using a grooved board or rolling pin. Cut out one petal using the 'head' petal cutter (461). Moisten and insert a 26-gauge wire into at least half the length of the petal.

5 Vein the petal using the amaryllis veiner. Place the petal on a pad and soften the edges using a medium celstick. (Some of the bauhinias have petals with very frilled edges, while others don't – decide which you prefer!) Pinch the back of the petal from the base to the tip, using your finger and thumb, to create a central vein. Dry for about 30 minutes.

6 Cut out two more petals with the 'arms' cutter (460), and two with the 'legs' cutter (462). Repeat steps 4 and 5 with these four petals, and leave to dry for 30 minutes.

COLOURING AND ASSEMBLY

7 Dust each petal with pink and fuchsia using a 5mm (¼ in) flat-headed brush, and working from the edges down towards the base. Over-dust with a little plum, then, working with aubergine, dust the base of each petal, making the colour on the 'head' petal much stronger and extending it further down the petal.

8 Paint a series of lines in a fan formation on the 'head' petal only (some species have all plain petals) using cyclamen liquid colour and a fine paintbrush.

9 Tape the petals around the pistil and stamens, using ½-width floristry tape. Start with the 'head' petal, and attach the 'arms' on either side, slightly behind the 'head', and then attach the 'legs' at the base of the 'arms'. As the paste is still quite damp, you can now gently re-position any of the petals.

BRACT

10 Roll out some pale green paste and cut out an arrowhead shape with a scalpel. Place on a pad and soften the edges with a celstick. Using a dresden tool, draw a series of veins on the paste.

11 Moisten the bract and attach to the back of the flower, wrapping the base around the stem. Dust with a little primrose and moss mixed together.

LEAVES

12 Roll out some mid-green paste using a grooved board or rolling pin. Cut out the leaves freehand using a sharp scalpel; they are oval in shape with a deep rounded 'V' removed from the tip. Insert a moistened 26-gauge or 24-gauge wire into each leaf. Vein using the black bryony veiner, and soften the edges with a large celstick. Pinch down the centre to reinforce the central vein. Allow to dry until firm enough to handle.

13 Dust each leaf with dark green and holly/ivy. Glaze using a ½ glaze, allow to dry, and then remove the colour on each vein using a scalpel.

Chinese Hibiscus

There are many different colour variations of this very showy flower, including white, yellow, pink, orange and red. As the name implies, the plant originates from southern China.

Materials

Fine and small white stamens
20, 24 and 26-gauge wires
Watermelon, red, aubergine,
dark green and holly/ivy petal
dust (blossom tint)
Clear alcohol (gin or vodka)
White and mid-green flower
paste
Poppy paste colouring
Mimosa-coloured pollen dust
½ glaze (see page 10)

Equipment

Pale green and white floristry
tape
Hibiscus petal veiner (GI)
Jem plastic trumpet-shaped
former (optional)
Rose calyx cutter (R11b)
Daisy cutters (108, 109)
Hibiscus leaf veiners (GI)

STAMENS AND PISTIL

1 Tape five small white stamens on to a 24-gauge wire using ¼-width white floristry tape. Paint the stamens with red petal dust mixed with a little alcohol. This forms the pistil.

2 Colour some white flower paste with poppy paste colouring to a paler shade than you want the finished flower to be. Shape a little of this coloured paste into a small ball, and thread it on to the wire so that the ball is just below the stamens. Work the paste between your finger and thumb, gradually pulling the paste down the wire to form a very slender shape, the base of which, in a real flower, is sometimes slightly broader. The total length should measure at least the length of one of the petals (although it is more usual for it to be a little longer). Pinch off any excess paste. Bend the whole piece to form a gentle curved shape.

3 Before the paste has a chance to dry, cut lots of fine stamens into short lengths and insert into the top part of the paste, just below the pistil. Try to cover a short length of approximately 2cm (¾ in) with the stamens. Allow to dry just a little.

4 Dust the paste and stamens with watermelon and red to add depth to the flower. Moisten the tips of the stamens with egg white and dip them gently into some mimosa-coloured pollen dust. Try to avoid getting pollen on the pistil.

PETALS

5 Roll out some of the poppy-coloured paste using a grooved rolling pin or board, remembering that the petals should be fairly 'fleshy'. Using the flat back side of the top half of the petal veiner, press down on top of the paste to leave an indented outline on the surface. Using a sharp scalpel, cut around the shape.

6 Insert a moistened 26-gauge white wire into the thick central ridge, inserting it to approximately half the length of the petal.

7 Place the petal in the double-sided petal veiner. Press down firmly, but be careful as this veiner has very strong veining. Remove the petal and place it back on the board. Using a cocktail stick (toothpick) or a tiny celstick, frill the edges of the petal. Some flowers have very frilly edges; others do not, so decide which you prefer. Make four more petals in exactly the same way.

8 Pinch down the centre of the backs of the petals to reinforce the central vein. Allow to dry over a gentle curve or in a plastic trumpet-shaped former, until firm enough to handle.

COLOURING AND ASSEMBLY

9 Dust from the base of each petal, gradually fading the colour as you reach the outer edges. Start with watermelon, and then over-dust with a little red, especially at the base. The back of each petal should be paler than the front.

10 At the very base of the petals there is usually a dark red, shiny patch. Mix a little alcohol with some red and aubergine petal dust and paint

the very base of each petal. Dip the base in a ½ glaze if you wish to achieve the shiny finish. Shake off the excess, and leave to dry.

11 Tape the petals around the stamens with ½-width green floristry tape, overlapping them a little.

CALYX

12 The hibiscus has a double calyx. To make the first one, roll out some mid-green paste, leaving the centre slightly thicker. (You could use a mexican hat board for this.) Cut out the shape using a rose calyx cutter. Broaden each of the sepals a little, and then place the calyx on a pad. Soften the edges with a celstick and draw down a central vein on each sepal with a dresden tool.

13 Moisten the centre and each sepal with egg white, and thread on to the back of the flower, trying to position each sepal slightly over a join. (This calyx should fit quite tightly against the back of the flower.)

14 The second calyx is cut out with a daisy cutter (109), then treated in exactly the

same way as the first calyx. Position on the base of the first calyx, curling the sepals back.

15 Dust both of the calyces with dark green and holly/ivy.

BUDS

16 Larger buds are formed from a cone of flower paste coloured to match the petals. Insert a short length of taped 20-gauge wire into the broad end.

17 To give the impression of petals, the easiest method is to use a 'cage' made from five 24-gauge wires (see page 10). Open the wires up and insert the bud, tip first. Close the wires into the base, keeping them as evenly spaced as possible. Using your finger and thumb, pinch out some paste between the wires. Open up the cage and remove the bud. Twist the sections of the bud together in a clockwise movement to form a neat spiral effect. Dust the bud with watermelon and a little red petal dust.

18 Add a double calyx as described for the flower (see steps 12–15 above).

19 Smaller buds are made in the same way using green paste. Mark smaller buds with a 'cage' of wires, pinching a ridge on each section between the wires. Remove the cage but do not twist the bud as before. Instead, cut into the top of the bud using a pair of fine scissors, following the line of each of the sepals. Add only the second calyx as described above, but using a smaller daisy cutter (108). Dust with dark green and holly/ivy.

LEAVES

20 Roll out some mid-green paste using a grooved rolling pin or board. Cut out a basic leaf shape using a sharp scalpel. Insert a moistened 26-gauge or 24-gauge wire, depending on the size of the leaf.

21 Vein the leaves using the hibiscus leaf veiners, pressing firmly to give the full leaf impression. After removing each leaf from the veiner, cut the edges using scissors to give a slightly jagged effect. Work a little more on these edges using the broad end of the dresden tool. Place on a pad and soften the edges a little more using a large celstick. Allow to dry just a little.

22 Dust with dark green petal dust, and then over-dust with holly/ivy. Use a touch of aubergine on the very edge of each leaf. Dip into a ½ glaze, shake off excess, and leave to dry.

Note

Some species of *Hibiscus* have variegated foliage, which can give an alternative, softer appearance to the plant.

Caladium

Although the caladiums are native to Central and South America, there are many cultivars, and it is widely available now as a pot plant. It is a useful foliage to use in arrangements because of its size and unusual markings.

Materials

Ivory flower paste
18, 20 and 22-gauge wires
Dark green, holly/ivy, primrose, moss, apricot, coral and red petal dust (blossom tint)
Clear alcohol (gin or vodka)
Cornflour
¼ glaze (see page 10)

Equipment

Caladium leaf cutters
Pale green floristry tape
Caladium veiners (GI)

1 Roll out some flower paste leaving a slightly thicker area down the centre. Cut out a leaf. Tape over a wire with ¼-width floristry tape. Moisten the end and insert it into the leaf.

2 Place the leaf between the double-sided veiners and press firmly. Remove the leaf and place it on a pad. Soften the edges with the rounded end of a large celstick, and pinch firmly down the centre of the leaf.

Allow to dry draped over the edge of the pad.

COLOURING

3 Mix together some holly/ivy and dark green petal dusts, and dilute with a little clear alcohol. Paint in the main markings following the veins on the leaf. Paint in the finer markings and a border around the inner edge.

4 Using a mixture of primrose, dark green, moss,

holly/ivy and a lot of cornflour, dust a little colour on to the leaf surface. Using the darker greens, dust from the edge of the leaf to the border line.

5 The leaf can be left green and white, or you can create some very strong colouring. The leaves illustrated are coloured with a mixture of coral and apricot, and then over-dusted with a touch of red. Glaze using a ¼ glaze.

Madagascar Flamboyant

Flamboyant by name, flamboyant by nature, *Delonix regia* is one of the most spectacular tropical flowering trees with its huge red flowers and lacy bright green foliage. Its size has been scaled down here to make it more suitable to use on cakes.

Materials

Tiny seed-head stamens
Red paste colouring
Clear alcohol (gin or vodka)
24, 28 and 30-gauge wires
White and holly/ivy flower paste
Red, white, spring green, lemon and moss petal dust (blossom tint)
¼ glaze (see page 10)

Equipment

Pale green floristry tape
Nasturtium petal cutter (447)
Orchid or other veiner with fan-formation markings
Ceramic silk veining tool
Small stencil brush (optional)
Nasturtium calyx cutter (448)

STAMENS AND PISTIL

1 Paint the length of ten stamens with red paste colouring diluted with a little alcohol or water. The tips can be a dark burgundy (in new flowers) or white (in more mature specimens).

2 To make the pistil, tape over a short length of 30-gauge wire with ¼-width green floristry tape. Bend gently, and then tape the stamens around the pistil, making sure that the tips of the stamens are fractionally higher than the top of the pistil.

FLOWERS

3 Colour some flower paste a slightly paler red than you want the flower to be. Roll out the paste using a grooved board or rolling pin. Cut out four petals using the nasturtium petal cutter.

4 Insert a moistened 28-gauge wire into the central ridge of each petal, making sure the wire is inserted to at least half the length of the petal.

5 Roll the base of each petal between your finger and thumb to form a more slender shape. Place each petal on the orchid veiner and press very firmly to give a full impression. Remove from the veiner and place back on the board with the veined side facing you.

6 Using the broad end of a dresden tool, frill the edges of the petals to create a slightly jagged frilled effect. Frill over this area using the ceramic silk veining tool. Pinch each petal down the centre and curve very slightly. Allow to dry for approximately 30 minutes.

7 Make a fifth petal using white flower paste, following the above instructions. When you frill this petal, try to broaden the rounded part of the petal as this tends to be slightly larger.

COLOURING AND ASSEMBLY

8 Dust the red petals from the edges with red petal dust. If the petals have dried too much and the colour is not sticking very well, steam the petals (see page 10), and then re-dust.

9 Paint some darker markings on each petal using red paste colouring mixed with a little clear alcohol. The marking should be at the centre of each petal, following the direction of the veining. Dip into a ¼ glaze, shake off excess, and leave to dry.

10 The white petal has lots of markings which can either be painted on individually with a fine paintbrush, or sprayed on with a stencil brush (as for the flowers illustrated). Dab the brush in the darker red colouring that has been used for the other petals, then hold the brush above the petal and draw your finger over the bristles, spraying the colour on to the surface of the petal. (Be careful not to use too much liquid as this will give very large marks.)

11 As well as the small markings there are also some lines which should be painted on with a fine brush. Dust the base of the petal with lemon petal dust. Dip into a ¼ glaze, shake off excess, and dry.

12 Tape the white petal on to the stamens and pistil. Add the remaining four petals and, if the paste is still damp, curl the edges a little more if needed.

CALYX

13 Roll out some green paste fairly thickly and cut out a shape using the nasturtium calyx cutter, retaining the paste in the cutter after cutting. Roll out some red paste and, without removing the green paste, cut out another red calyx shape. The two pieces should hold together quite well. Remove the calyx from the cutter and if the two colours have not stuck together add a little egg white.

14 Place the calyx on a pad with the red side on top. Hollow out the sepals using the broad end of the dresden tool. It is important that the edges of each sepal curl inwards.

15 Moisten the centre of the calyx and position it on the back of the flower, making sure each sepal is positioned in between a petal.

16 Dust the inside of the calyx with a little red petal dust, and the back with spring green.

BUD

17 Roll a ball of green paste into a cone and insert a hooked, moistened 24-gauge wire into the pointed end. Pinch the paste down on to the wire a little. Divide the surface into five using a 'cage' made from five 24-gauge wires (see page 10). Remove the cage and pinch a sharp point at the tip of the bud.

18 Dust the bud with spring green and a touch of moss. Dip into a ¼ glaze, shake off any excess, and leave to dry, then tape over the stem with ½-width green floristry tape.

LEAVES

19 The leaves are very fine; here I have simply tried to represent them. The leaves tend to open when the tree has fairly mature flowers on each branch.

20 Cut lots of pieces of ¼-width green tape. Twist each piece of tape back on to itself to make fine strands.

21 Tape the first strand on to a 30-gauge wire. Continue to add more strands until you have created a reasonable length. Make several pieces and then tape these together on to a 24-gauge wire using ½-width tape. Dust with moss green and plenty of spring green.

Cape Leadwort

This plant *(Plumbago auriculata)* is a favourite choice for the tropical garden or conservatory. Occasionally white forms are seen, but most are pale to mid blue.

Equipment

Harebell cutter
Rose leaf veiner (GI)
Pale green floristry
tape

Materials

White and pale green flower paste
28-gauge wires
Bluebell, lavender, deep purple, skintone, white, spring green and dark green petal dust (blossom tint)
Clear alcohol (gin or vodka)
¼ glaze (see page 10)

FLOWER

1 Roll a small ball of white paste into a fine teardrop shape. Pinch out the base to form a pedestal. Place the flat base down on a board and roll out the paste very finely using a small celstick.

2 Cut out the flower using the harebell cutter. Before you remove the paste from the cutter, rub your thumb across the edge to make sure you have cleanly cut edges to the petals.

3 Place the flower on a pad and soften the edges using the rounded end of the small celstick. Open up the centre of the flower using the point of a cocktail stick (toothpick). Vein the centre of each petal using a dresden tool. Insert a moistened 28-gauge wire. Work the back of the flower between your finger and thumb to form a very fine, slender tube.

4 To form the calyx, attach a piece of green paste to the base of the flower and snip several times with fine scissors.

BUD

5 Roll a small ball of white paste into a teardrop shape and insert a moistened 28-gauge wire. Work the paste between your finger and thumb to form a very slender bud. Add a calyx as described for the flower.

COLOURING

6 Dust the flowers and buds with a very pale mixture of bluebell, white and lavender, making the centre of each flower slightly darker. Mix a little of the flower colour with deep purple and a little clear alcohol. Using a very fine paintbrush, paint a line down the centre of each petal. Dust the calyx with skintone petal dust.

LEAVES

7 Roll a ball of green paste into a teardrop and insert a moistened 28-gauge wire into the pointed end. Flatten the teardrop and then place into the rose veiner, pressing firmly to thin the leaf out. Place the leaf on a pad and soften the back using the rounded end of the small celstick.

8 Dust with spring green and a touch of dark green. Glaze using a ¼ glaze.

9 Tape the buds and flowers into clumps, and then tape the leaves in twos and threes down the stem. Tape smaller stems together to form a larger one. Dust the stems with the greens and a little skintone.

Blue Gum Blossom

The gum blossom *(Eucalyptus globulus)* pictured below has been made with a lot of artistic licence! It is, however, great fun to make.

Materials

20, 24, 26 and 28-gauge wires
Lemon, maize and white cotton embroidery thread
White and pale holly/ivy flower paste
Lemon, cream, cornflower blue, white, dark green, spring green, holly/ivy, primrose, champagne, aubergine, nutkin and black petal dust (blossom tint)
Semolina
Couscous
¼ glaze (see page 10)

Equipment

Beige and pale green floristry tape
Emery board
Tweezers
Leaf templates (see page 141)

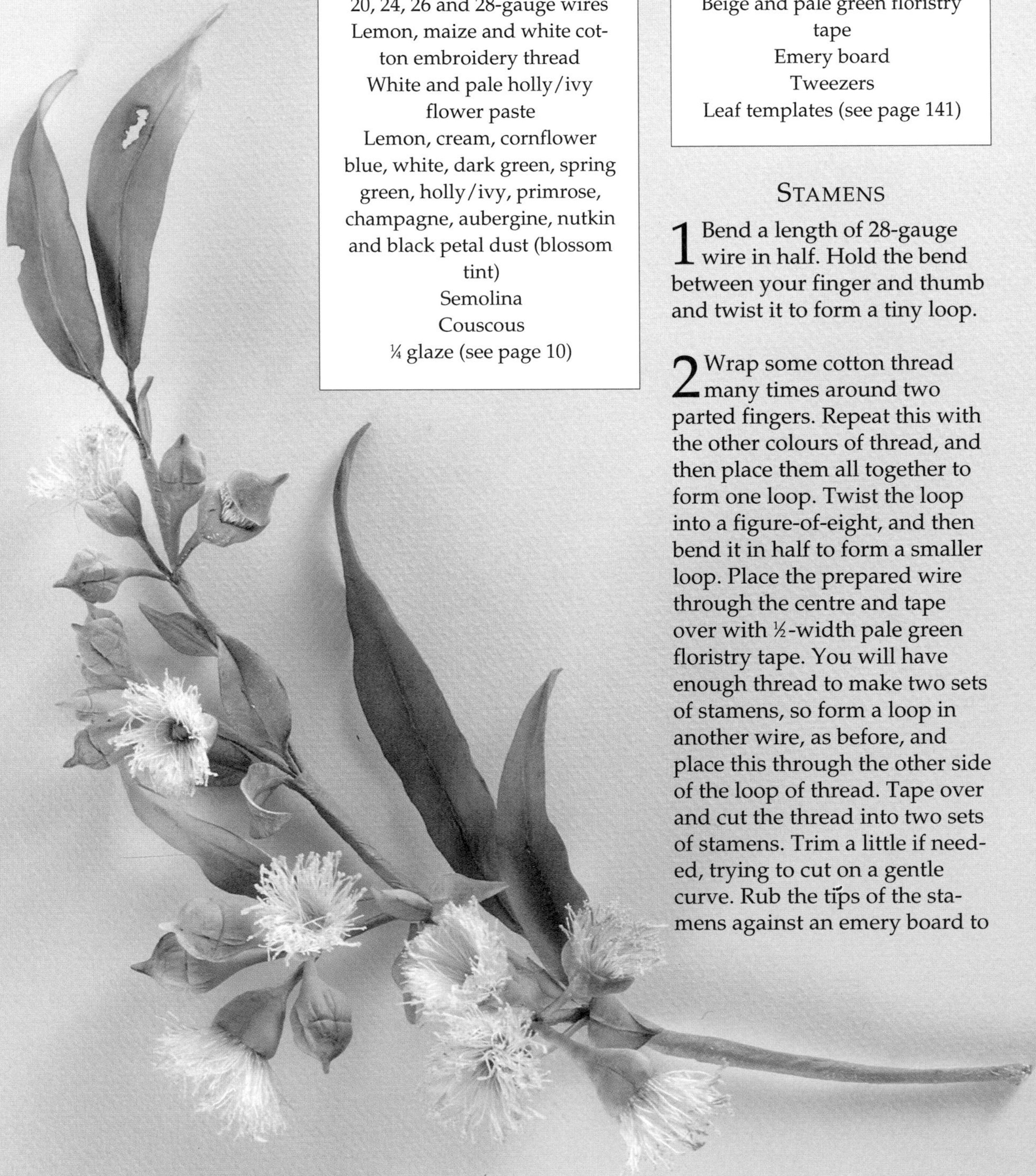

Stamens

1 Bend a length of 28-gauge wire in half. Hold the bend between your finger and thumb and twist it to form a tiny loop.

2 Wrap some cotton thread many times around two parted fingers. Repeat this with the other colours of thread, and then place them all together to form one loop. Twist the loop into a figure-of-eight, and then bend it in half to form a smaller loop. Place the prepared wire through the centre and tape over with ½-width pale green floristry tape. You will have enough thread to make two sets of stamens, so form a loop in another wire, as before, and place this through the other side of the loop of thread. Tape over and cut the thread into two sets of stamens. Trim a little if needed, trying to cut on a gentle curve. Rub the tips of the stamens against an emery board to

create a little bulk. Attach a tiny piece of white flower paste over the loop of wire in the centre, and form into a point.

CALYX

3 Roll a ball of white paste into a cone shape and thin out the base into a tube. Open up and thin the rounded end using a celstick. Moisten the centre and thread the stamens through. Pinch the calyx firmly around the stamens. Using tweezers, pinch the calyx into four sections. Pinch the centre of each section with your finger and thumb to form a ridge.

4 Dust the calyx with a mixture of dark green, cornflower blue and white. Overdust with black and nutkin.

5 Dust the stamens to various depths using a mixture of primrose and lemon petal dust. The pollen on the stamens is made by mixing semolina and

couscous with primrose, cream, champagne and lemon. Brush a little egg white on a board, dip the stamens in it, then dip in the 'pollen' mixture.

BUDS

6 Roll a small ball of paste into a cone shape and insert a moistened 26-gauge wire. Pinch a tiny point at the tip and then divide the cone into two using a scalpel to form the 'lid'. Pinch with tweezers as for the flower, this time continuing the indents on to the lid. Work the base of the cone down on to the wire. Dust as for the calyx.

7 To make a half-open bud, simply form a small bunch of thread on the end of a 28-gauge wire. Model the calyx as for the flower, and attach, and then model a separate piece to form the lid. Trim the stamens so that they are fairly short, and then attach the lid using egg white. Dust as before.

LEAVES

8 Roll out some pale green paste using a grooved board. Cut out the leaves using a scalpel and templates. Insert either a 26-gauge or 24-gauge wire. Soften the edges and draw down a central vein. Pinch the whole length of the leaf into shape and allow to firm up.

9 Dust with dark green, holly/ivy and white, adding a little aubergine on the very edges. Paint the central vein to make it paler. Glaze using a ¼ glaze. Make a variety of sizes, including some very small leaves to use at the base of each flower cluster. The smaller leaves are coloured to more of a fresh spring green. Tape pieces together on to 20-gauge wire using beige floristry tape.

Trumpet Vine

There are two species of Trumpet Vine (*Campsis*), one from the eastern United States and the other from China and Japan. I have based my vine on both! The flowers and leaves are large; I have scaled them down to make them suitable to use on cakes.

Materials

20, 24, 26 and 33-gauge wires
White, peach and holly/ivy flower paste
Tangerine, red, coral, aubergine, lemon, dark green and moss petal dust (blossom tint)
½ glaze (see page 10)

Equipment

Fine pliers
Pale green floristry tape
Large blossom cutters (474, 475)
Ceramic silk veining tool (HP)
Rose calyx cutters (R11, R12)
Large and small hydrangea veiners (GI)

STAMENS AND PISTIL

1 Cut four short lengths of 33-gauge wire. Bend a small closed hook in one end of each. Holding the hook halfway along, bend it again to form a 'T'-bar. Attach a tiny sausage of white flower paste to the end and pinch slightly at the centre. Dust with lemon petal dust to form the pollen.

2 To make the pistil, attach a ball of white paste on the end of a 33-gauge wire, and work it between your finger and thumb until it covers the wire in a thin layer. Divide the top end into two. Dust with lemon and tangerine, leaving the end paler.

3 Tape the four stamens around the pistil using ½-width floristry tape. Tape a couple of lengths of 24-gauge wire on to the stamens to give a little more support.

FLOWER

4 Roll a large ball of peach-coloured paste into a cone shape. Pinch out the broad end of the cone, and then place it on a board. Roll out the broad end of the cone with a celstick, remembering that this flower is very 'fleshy' and it is important to work with the paste fairly thick.

5 Cut out the flower using a large blossom cutter. Cut out a 'V' shape from in between each petal using a scalpel.

6 Open up the centre of the flower using the pointed end of a small celstick. Work the sides of the flower against the stick, to thin it down a little.

7 Place the flower against your fingers with one petal over your index finger. Roll and frill the edges of each petal using the ceramic silk veining tool.

8 Moisten the base of the stamens and pull them through the centre of the flower. Pinch the base of the flower to secure it in place. Allow to dry a little before colouring.

9 Dust from the edges of each petal with tangerine, coral and then a little red. Dust aubergine deep in the flower centre. The back of the flower is dusted with lemon from the base, and then with the orange

mixture from the edges of the petals, gradually blending into the lemon.

CALYX

10 Roll out a piece of green paste, leaving the centre slightly thicker. Cut out the calyx using the large rose calyx cutter. Broaden and elongate each of the sepals using a celstick. Place on a pad and draw down a central vein using the fine end of a dresden tool. Moisten the centre and position on the back of the flower, closing the sepals around tightly. Dust with a little moss green.

BUDS

11 To make small buds, attach small cones of green paste on to 26-gauge wires. Divide the surface into five using a scalpel or a 'cage' (see page 10).

12 To make larger buds, attach a large cone of peach paste on to a 24-gauge wire, inserting the wire into the fine end. Pinch the broad end five times between your finger and thumb to form the petals.

Moisten the centre and then fold the petals back in over the top part of the cone. Add a calyx as described for the flower. Dust with the tangerine, coral and red petal dust. For smaller buds, use the smaller calyx cutter.

LEAVES

13 Roll out some green flower paste using a grooved board or rolling pin. Cut out basic leaf shapes using a scalpel. Insert a moistened 26-gauge wire into at least half the length of each leaf.

14 Vein using the hydrangea veiners, pressing firmly together. After veining, cut into the edge of each leaf using a pair of fine scissors to give a jagged effect. Soften the edges a little and allow to firm up before colouring.

15 Dust with dark green and over-dust with moss. Dust the edges with aubergine and red mixed together. Dip into a ½ glaze, shake off the excess, and leave to dry.

16 Tape the leaves together in groups. On the real flower, the leaves usually grow in groups of five, seven or nine, but smaller groups of three can be made if needed.

Bauhinias in Rhapsody

This beautiful cake with its dramatic spray of exotic bauhinia would make an impressive centrepiece for a birthday or anniversary. The side design has been kept very simple in form to complement and not detract from the floral spray.

Materials

23cm (9 in) heart-shaped cake
Apricot glaze
1kg (2lb) almond paste (marzipan)
Clear alcohol (kirsch or vodka)
1.5kg (3lb) shell pink sugarpaste
White royal icing
Fine willow green ribbon to trim cake
Green velvet ribbon to trim board
Pale green flower paste
Dark green, white and pink petal dust (blossom tint)

Equipment

32cm (13 in) heart-shaped cake board
Sugarpaste smoothers
No. 1 piping tube (tip)
Simple leaf cutters (229–232)
Pale green floristry tape
Wire cutters
Posy pick

Flowers

7 stems of trailing ivy (see page 22)
about 5 stems of Chinese jasmine with foliage (see page 20)
3 bauhinia flowers (see page 58)
3 large ivy leaves (see page 22)

PREPARATION

1 Brush the cake with apricot glaze and cover with almond paste. Leave to dry overnight. Moisten the cake with alcohol, and cover the cake and board separately with sugarpaste, using sugarpaste smoothers to achieve a good finish. Position the cake on the cake board and allow to dry.

2 Pipe a snail's trail around the base of the cake using white royal icing and a no. 1 piping tube. Fasten willow green ribbon around the cake just above the snail's trail, and attach velvet ribbon to the board edge.

SIDE DECORATION

3 Roll out some pale green flower paste very finely and using squashed simple leaf cutters (see page 21), cut out jasmine leaves in various sizes. Place the leaves on a pad and soften the edges with a celstick. Draw down a central vein on each leaf with a dresden tool. Moisten the back of each leaf and position in groups on the cake board and sides of the cake. Use a template to mark the leaf positions first, if needed.

4 Mix some dark green petal dust with a little alcohol. Using a fine paintbrush, paint the main and smaller stems on the cake and board. Darken the leaves using a larger brush, and then, working with white petal dust and alcohol, paint some jasmine buds into the design. Add a little pink to areas of the design, especially on the buds.

SPRAY

5 Use the trailing ivy and jasmine stems to create the curved outline of the spray. Bend the stems at an angle of 90° to create a handle for the spray, and tape together with ½-width floristry tape. Trim away any excess wire.

6 Add the three bauhinia flowers, positioning them, if possible, so they each face in a different direction. Tape the best and largest flower in the centre, slightly higher than the other two, to form the focal point of the spray. Add the larger ivy leaves, and more stems of jasmine, if required, to fill in any gaps.

7 Insert a plastic posy pick into the cake, and then insert the handle of the spray into the posy pick. Gently bend and rearrange the flowers a little, if needed, to complete the display.

A Splash of the Exotic

This stunning two-tiered wedding cake is reminiscent of the Caribbean, making it the ideal centrepiece for any couple planning to honeymoon, or indeed marry, in such an exotic location.

Materials

15cm (6 in) and 20cm (8 in) heart-shaped cakes
Apricot glaze
1.5kg (3lb) almond paste (marzipan)
Clear alcohol (kirsch or vodka)
2.5kg (5lb) sugarpaste, coloured with a little poppy and mulberry paste colouring
Fine pale blue ribbon to trim cakes
Flesh-coloured ribbon to trim boards

Equipment

Sugarpaste smoothers
20cm (8 in) and 30cm (12 in) heart-shaped cake boards
Pale green floristry tape
Fine pliers
Wire cutters
Piece of conditioned drift-wood, 28cm (11 in) in height
2 posy picks
Double-sided carpet tape

Flowers

2 hibiscus flowers (see page 60)
14 hibiscus leaves, various sizes (see page 62)
5 small and 3 large hibiscus buds (see page 62)
12 caladium leaves, various sizes (see page 63)
3 bud clusters and 5 flower clusters of cape leadwort (see page 67)

PREPARATION

1 Brush the cakes with apricot glaze and cover with almond paste. Allow to dry overnight. Moisten the almond paste with clear alcohol and cover with sugarpaste, using smoothers to achieve a good finish. Cover the cake boards with sugarpaste and place the cakes on top, making sure you have a neat join between the base of each cake and its board. Attach a band of fine blue ribbon around the base of each cake. Attach flesh-coloured ribbon around the cake boards.

2 Tape the flowers and foliage into two modern-style sprays, using the leaves to form the basic shapes. Bend the stems at an angle of 90° to form handles to the sprays. Tape over with floristry tape and trim away excess wires.

CAKE STAND

3 The cake stand has been made using a piece of conditioned driftwood purchased from a florist's shop. The top of the wood needs to have a smooth surface to hold the cake, so cut it to the required angle. Push a posy pick into each cake, positioning one to the right of the top cake, and the other to the left of the bottom cake.

4 Position the smaller cake on the stand using double-sided carpet tape to hold it in place (see Note).

5 Place the bottom tier in front of the base of the driftwood. Once the two cakes are in position, insert the handles of the floral sprays into the posy picks, and gently bend and arrange the flowers decoratively on the cakes.

Note

If you are worried that the small cake will be too heavy to rest securely on top of the drift-wood stand, use a polystyrene dummy cake for the display and provide a separate cake for cutting.

Flamboyant Festive Cake

I love working with very strong, bold colours and Christmas provides the perfect opportunity. This cake, with its richly coloured flamboyant flowers, would make a stunning centrepiece for a Christmas table. The cake has a very unusual speckled surface which complements the flower sprays rather than detracts from them.

Materials

20cm (8 in) teardrop cake
Apricot glaze
750g (1½lb) almond paste (marzipan)
Clear alcohol (kirsch or vodka)
1kg (2lb) champagne sugarpaste
Fine red ribbon to trim cake
Green velvet ribbon to trim board
Dark green, red and gold petal dust (blossom tint)

Equipment

Sugarpaste smoothers
25cm (10 in) teardrop cake board
Stencil brush
Florists' staysoft
Glue gun and non-toxic glue stick
2 small round cake cards

Flowers

2 flamboyant sprays (see page 79)
25cm (10 in) twisted twig garland

PREPARATION

1 Brush the cake with apricot glaze, cover with almond paste and allow to dry overnight. Moisten the cake with clear alcohol and cover with champagne sugarpaste, using sugarpaste smoothers to achieve a good finish. Cover the cake board separately with sugarpaste, and place the cake on top, making sure that you have a neat join between the base of the cake and the board. Allow to dry. Attach fine red ribbon around the base of the cake, and green velvet ribbon around the board edge.

2 To create the speckled effect, mix some green petal dust with a little clear alcohol. Dab the bristles of a stencil brush in the colour, aim the brush at the cake and rub the bristles firmly, splashing the cake with colour. Cover the whole of the cake and the board, and then repeat the process using red and gold colour.

ASSEMBLY

3 Position the cake into the centre of the twisted twig garland, lifting the cake at the back so that it rests on the garland and tilts forwards. For more tilt (and to protect the garland), raise the back of the cake on a lump of staysoft, if preferred.

4 Using the glue gun, stick a clump of staysoft on each of the small round cake cards. Secure the floral sprays in the staysoft, and position them next to the cake. (The staysoft should not come into contact with the cake.)

Flamboyant Candle Decoration

A Christmas cake has limited life, so using candles with the flower sprays before and after Christmas is a good idea. Simply remove the sprays and position them with the cake when needed!

Flowers

8 stems of large ivy (see page 22)
12 flamboyant flowers with buds and foliage (see page 64)
8 clumps of ivy berries, coloured gold (see Note), see page 123
6–8 clumps of long eucalyptus leaves with buds, coloured gold (see Note), see page 68

Equipment

18-gauge wires
Pale green floristry tape
Fine pliers
Wire cutters
25cm (10 in) pewter plate (or similar)
3 broad candles of various heights
Florists' staysoft
Broad red ribbon

FLORAL SPRAYS

1 Strengthen any of the flower stems, if necessary, by taping in 18-gauge wires. Start forming the outline of a large spray using five of the ivy stems. Bend each stem to an angle of 90° to form a handle before taping together with ½-width floristry tape. Introduce some full stems of flamboyant.

2 Add some more flamboyant (seven in all), spacing them to fill the main bulk of the spray. Try to use the largest and most attractive flower in the centre of the spray to form the focal point.

3 Add depth and interest to the spray by adding gold ivy berries and eucalyptus stems, slightly recessed in between the flamboyant flowers.

4 Wire up a similar spray with the remaining flowers to place on the other side of the arrangement.

ASSEMBLY

5 Group the candles together on a pewter plate and place a spray of flowers on either side, using florists' staysoft to hold them in place. Tie a bow of red ribbon and place it in front of the candles. (Before you light the candles, make sure the sugar flowers are not too close to the flames!)

Note

The easiest way to colour berries and buds gold is to spray them with gold spray paint.

Frog Down Under

This cake was inspired by a piece of work by the textile artist Annemieke Mein. I was so excited by her book, *The Art of Annemieke Mein* (Search Press/ Schwartz), that I wrote to ask her permission to use the frog design on a cake. She agreed, and here it is. My version does little justice to the original, but this is still my favourite cake in this book.

Materials

25cm (10 in) long octagonal cake
Apricot glaze
1kg (2lb) almond paste (marzipan)
Clear alcohol (kirsch or vodka)
1.5kg (3lb), plus 125g (4oz), white sugarpaste
Fine willow green ribbon, to trim cake
Baby maize ribbon, to trim board
125g (4oz) flower paste
Lemon, moss, holly/ivy, aubergine, dark green, white, black, brown, nutkin, primrose and skintone petal dust (blossom tint)
Green, pearl and gold lustre colours
Black paste colouring

Equipment

Sugarpaste smoothers
36cm (14 in) long octagonal cake board
Posy pick

Flowers

Long stem of eucalyptus with flowers (see page 68)

PREPARATION

1 Brush the cake with apricot glaze and cover with almond paste. Leave to dry overnight. Moisten the almond paste with clear alcohol and cover with 1.5kg (3lb) white sugarpaste, using sugarpaste smoothers to achieve a good finish. Cover the board with sugarpaste and place the cake on top. Allow to dry thoroughly. Attach fine willow green ribbon around the base of the cake, and baby maize ribbon around the board edge.

BAS RELIEF FROG

2 Trace the frog design on page 142 on to tracing or greaseproof paper, then scribe the design on to the surface of the cake.

3 Mix together the remaining 125g (4oz) sugarpaste with the flower paste to form a modelling paste. Roll out the paste so that it is large enough to cut out the whole of the frog. Place the template on top of the paste, and scribe the design on to it. Using a scalpel, cut around the design.

4 Moisten the design on the cake surface with a little alcohol. Carefully lift the cut-out frog and place it on top of the cake so it fits into the scribed outline.

5 Certain areas of the design will need building up with more paste to give the frog a two-dimensional look. For example, the frog's stomach area, head, upper legs and calves will need to be built up. To do this, simply place extra

pieces of paste on to the surface and blend the edges into the piece beneath using your finger and a dresden tool.

6 To create the texture of the frog's body, roll tiny balls of paste and attach them all over the frog's torso up to its lips. Flatten and indent each ball to help give the appearance of scales.

7 Build up the branch so that it is slightly higher than most of the figure. Add an extension to the branch to hang over the edge of the cake. Again, simply blend the two pieces of paste together. Support the branch extension with a large piece of sponge until it is dry. Texture the whole branch with the fine end of the dresden tool, using long strokes.

8 Paint the branch with nutkin and brown petal dust mixed with a little alcohol. Shade in areas of the branch using a more concentrated mixture; add depth by mixing in a touch of black petal dust. Leave to dry.

9 Once the branch is dry you can start work on the frog's

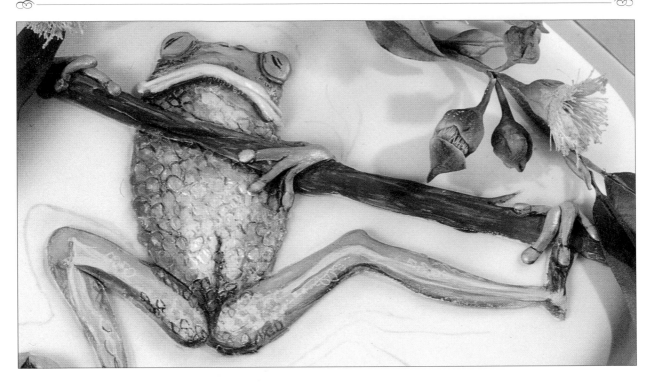

hands and feet. Working with the modelling paste again, form each of the fingers and toes separately, joining them together when you put them in place. Indent the joint just above the rounded tip.

10 Build up the lips and indent down the centre using the fine end of the dresden tool. Roll a fine strip of paste to fit underneath each of the frog's eyes.

COLOURING

11 Paint the frog with a little holly/ivy, white and

primrose mixed with alcohol, leaving the lips white. Shade in the edges of the frog heavier on one side than the other. At this stage you can also add finer detail. Paint over the base of the torso, inner parts of the legs and just underneath the lips with white.

12 Using lemon, white and a touch of skintone, paint in the eyes. Once they are dry, over-paint with some gold lustre colour. Paint in the pupils with a little black paste colouring.

13 Paint areas of the frog with some more of the gold lustre colour. The white areas are painted over with pearl lustre colour.

FLOWERS AND FOLIAGE

14 Using a very pale muted green, dust around the frog on the surface of the cake. Using a finer brush, paint in some fine movement lines with a mid-green mixture diluted with a touch of alcohol. Paint some leaves on the sides of the cake.

15 Position the eucalyptus stem on the cake's surface, inserting the end into a posy pick at the back of the cake. (You might find you have to stuff the pick with paste to help hold the stem in place.)

16 Finally, cut out some large leaves using a template made from the outline on page 141. I have made the base leaf much paler than the other two to help with the two-dimensional effect. Vein the leaves with the dresden tool, or use a tiny dressmakers' wheel to give the impression of stitch marks. Dust each leaf with various shades of dark green, holly/ivy and white. Catch the edge of each leaf with a touch of aubergine. Using a little clear alcohol and some dark green, paint over the stitch marks to emphasize the veins. Using fine scissors, cut some 'insect nibbles' out of some of the leaves.

17 Moisten the back of each leaf and position on the cake as shown in the main photograph (page 81).

Trumpet Vine Christening Cake

This delightful cake, with its bright colour and strong shape, makes a stunning alternative to a more traditional pastel-coloured cake. The trumpet vine flowers during the summer months, making it the perfect choice for a baby born at that time of year. The baby is represented by a blossom fairy, sleeping happily in a leaf hammock!

Materials

25cm (10 in) scalloped oval cake
Apricot glaze
1kg (2lb) almond paste (marzipan)
Clear alcohol (kirsch or vodka)
1.5kg (3lb) white sugarpaste
Fine bright orange ribbon to trim cake
Green velvet ribbon to trim board
18 and 33-gauge wires
White, green, peach and flesh-coloured flower paste
Tangerine, red, cream, nutkin, apricot, cornflower blue, lavender, dark green and white petal dust (blossom tint)
Blue and pearl lustre colours
½ glaze (see page 10)
Fine lace-making thread

Equipment

36cm (14 in) scalloped oval cake board
Pale green floristry tape
2 posy picks
Tiny baby mould
Tiny blossom cutter
Tropical and tiny butterfly cutters (HH)
Leaf template (see page 141)
Large hydrangea leaf veiner (GI)

Flowers

1 long and 1 short stem of trumpet vine (see page 70)

head using your chosen colour. (I have used a mixture of cream and nutkin brown.)

4 Colour the cheeks with a little apricot petal dust. Using a fine paintbrush, paint on the eyelashes (dark brown) and colour in the lips (apricot).

PREPARATION

1 Brush the cake with apricot glaze, cover with almond paste and allow to dry overnight. Moisten the almond paste with clear alcohol and cover with white sugarpaste. Cover the cake board with white sugarpaste and place the cake on top, making sure you have a neat join between the base of the cake and the board. Allow to dry overnight. Attach a fine band of orange ribbon around the base of the cake, and position a bow in each of the indents. Attach velvet ribbon around the board edge.

2 Strengthen the stems of the trumpet vine, if necessary, by taping an extra 18-gauge wire alongside each stem. Arrange the flowers on the cake, inserting the end of each stem into a posy pick. You might have to fill the picks with paste to help hold the stems in place. Arrange some of the foliage on the cake's surface.

TRUMPET VINE FAIRY

3 Make a tiny baby using a mould and some flesh-coloured flower paste. Dust some hair on the baby's

5 The hat is made from peach-coloured paste and cut out using a tiny blossom cutter. Attach the hat to the baby's head using a touch of egg white. Paint the rim with blue lustre colour.

6 Cut out a pair of wings using a tiny butterfly cutter and some white flower paste. Glue them on to the baby's back. Paint the surface with a design using a mixture of cornflower blue and lavender petal dusts mixed with alcohol.

Leaf hammock

7 Roll out some green flower paste and cut out a leaf using a scalpel and a template made from the outline on page 141. Vein using the hydrangea veiner, and soften the edges using a large celstick.

8 Using a scriber, make a hole at each end of the leaf. Rest the leaf on a pad of foam rubber to help keep the curved shape, and leave to dry. Dust the leaf with dark green and glaze using a ½ glaze. Leave to dry.

9 Model a tiny pillow using white flower paste and cut out a small rectangle of peach paste. Frill the edges of both. Place the pillow on the leaf, then the baby and then cover the baby's body with the peach flower paste blanket, making sure that the wings are in full view.

10 Tie some fine lace-making thread through the holes in the leaf and dust it with some green petal dust. Place a large piece of sponge on top of the cake just below the curving stem of the trumpet vine. Place the hammock on top, and then tie the thread on to the buds or leaves. Gently remove the sponge.

Fantasy butterflies

11 Specimen butterflies could be made instead of fantasy ones, but I felt as the whole scene was one of fantasy they seemed more appropriate. Roll out some white flower paste on a grooved board, making sure the paste is very fine. Cut out the butterfly with your chosen cutter/veiner, and press the paste into the cutter to make sure that all the veins are marked on to the paste. Remove the paste, place it on a pad and gently soften the edges (do not frill them). Insert a 33-gauge wire into the underside of the body and dry the wings in a 'V' shape. (I find a piece of card bent into a 'V' shape holds the paste very well.) Repeat to make a second butterfly.

12 Paint and dust some markings on the butterfly wings and bodies using the lustre colours and a little alcohol.

13 Position the butterflies on the vine and cake, using the inserted 33-gauge wires to hold them in place.

Garden Flowers

THE GARDEN provides a constant source of inspiration and a never-ending supply of flowers to make; this section includes some of my favourites. I have a very small, untidy garden, but I still find that it gives me a huge amount of pleasure. Many garden flowers can be grouped together without much thought and still give a colourful, cheerful and at the same time informal arrangement.

Nasturtium

The nasturtium (*Tropaeolum majus*) is my favourite of all plants, and it is the first flower that I worked out how to make! The wild form, with orange flowers, is native to Peru where it is a strong-growing climbing plant. It has now been extensively cultivated, producing flowers in a wide range of colours.

Materials

Fine white stamens
18, 24, 26 and 28-gauge wires
Lemon, tangerine, red, aubergine, primrose, plum, dark green, holly/ivy, spring green and moss petal dust (blossom tint)
Nasturtium, pale melon and pale holly/ivy flower paste
Cyclamen or burgundy paste colouring
¼ and full glaze (see page 10)

Equipment

Pale green floristry tape
Nasturtium cutters (446–448)
Nasturtium petal and leaf veiners (GI)
Calyx cutter
Blossom cutter (F10)
Medium stephanotis cutter (566)
Fine pliers
Circle cutters (optional)

STAMENS AND PISTIL

1 Bend four fine stamens in half (to form eight) and add another stamen, which needs to be slightly longer than the others, to represent the pistil. Tape all of these together on to a 28-gauge wire using ¼-width floristry tape. Gently curl the stamens slightly, and then dust the tips with lemon petal dust.

PETALS

2 Roll out your chosen colour of paste (nasturtium has been used for the flowers illustrated) using a grooved rolling pin or board. Cut out three fringed (guitar-shaped) and two plain shapes using the nasturtium petal cutters.

3 Insert a moistened 28-gauge wire into the ridged area of each petal, making sure that the wire is inserted to at least half the length of the petal. Cover the petals with a sheet of plastic while you are not working on them to stop them drying out. Vein all of the petals.

4 Working first on the three fringed petals, use a cocktail stick (toothpick) to frill only the upper curve of each petal. Nasturtiums don't have a very frilly edge, but I find that they can look a little stiff if left plain. Using a pair of fine scissors, cut the middle section horizontally either side to represent fine hairs. (You will need to cut out small, deep 'V' shapes.) If these hairs are a little thick, place the paste back on the board and use the broad end of a dresden tool to flatten and thin the edges. Pinch the hairs from behind to display them on the upper surface. Allow the petals to firm up over a gentle curve.

5 Frill the edges of the remaining two petals, and then pinch them down the centre to reinforce the central vein. Allow these to firm up over a curve also.

COLOURING THE PETALS

6 Dust each petal from the edge towards the base using appropriate colours. (For the orange flowers, dust with tangerine and then a little red petal dust.) Colour the base of each petal with a touch of moss green.

7 The two plain petals have strong markings; paint these on using cyclamen or burgundy paste colour, a little water and a fine paintbrush. The lines radiate from the base, with the longest vein down the centre and those on either side getting shorter towards the edges.

8 Some varieties have burgundy shading; the petals illustrated here are dusted with a little aubergine petal dust on the centre.

ASSEMBLY

9 To assemble the flower, start by taping the two plain petals together with the stamens in front, curving towards them. Tape the three fringed petals in together, overlapping them as you feel necessary. As the flower is still slightly damp you can re-shape the edges if needed.

CALYX

10 Mix together a little pale melon and pale holly/ivy paste to create a creamy green, and roll a piece into a ball and then into a teardrop shape, trying to make this very fine as it represents the nectary which on the real flower is very slender. (The nectary, as the name implies, is where the nectar is stored.) Using your fingers and thumbs, pinch the larger end at the base to thin it out and turn it into the shape of a pointed hat. Place the 'hat' on the board and roll out the thinned area to make it a little finer.

11 Position the calyx cutter over the paste with one of the sepals closer to the nectary than the others, and then cut out the shape. Imagine the calyx as a person and broaden the 'arms' with a celstick. Place the calyx on a pad and soften the edges with a bone-end tool. Draw down a central vein on the inside of each sepal, and then,

using the pointed end of a cel-stick, open up the top of the nectary.

12 Moisten the inside of the calyx and then thread it on to the back of the flower so that the wire passes through the centre of the calyx and comes out just below the nectary, which should be positioned directly behind the join between the two plain petals. Stick down the sepals, making sure that each covers a join. Curl the nectary and then pinch the sides at the broad end with a pair of tweezers. Dust the tip of the nectary with a little moss and primrose petal dust.

BUDS

13 Roll out some paste the same colour as the flower, leaving the centre slightly thicker. (This can be done on a mexican hat board.) Cut out using the blossom cutter, and then gently frill the edges with a cocktail stick (toothpick).

14 Tape, hook and moisten a 24-gauge wire, and then thread on the blossom, pinching the thicker area of paste around the hook. Moisten the petals, and fold them together over the centre to form a neat bud. Make a calyx as for the flower, using the stephanotis cutter.

15 Tiny buds are made by forming a teardrop of pale melon paste, pinching the base to form a fine nectary, and marking the other end with a scalpel to form five sepals. Insert a hooked, moistened 28-gauge wire into the centre and pinch firmly to make sure it is secure. Curl the nectary and dust the bud with moss and primrose.

LEAVES

16 Tape over a 24-gauge or 26-gauge wire (depending on the size of the leaf), leaving a little at the end uncovered. Using pliers, hold the end of the wire and form an open round hook. Hold the hook halfway down and bend it so that it resembles a nail head.

17 Roll out some pale holly/ivy paste, leaving the centre slightly thicker. Cut out a leaf shape, either by using the veiner as a template and cutting with a scalpel, or using the circle cutters. Vein using the leaf veiners, and then soften the edges on a pad using a bone-end tool.

18 To fix the wire to the back of the leaf you can use egg white or edible glue (egg white mixed with flower paste to form a smooth consistency), but I find the most successful and quickest way is to heat up the end of the 'nail head' in a flame. As soon as the end turns red, place it on the centre of the

leaf (in the thick area). The join will be instant as the heat caramelizes the sugar and cools very quickly to give a fairly firm join. Whichever method you choose, remember that each leaf is secured to its wire in a very small area only, and some might drop off! If this happens, don't panic as they can always be attached again. Allow the leaves to dry before you colour them with petal dust.

COLOURING THE LEAVES

19 Dust the edges with a mixture of plum and aubergine. Colour the whole surface of the leaf, working from the centre, with dark green, and then over-dust with holly/ivy. Glaze the leaves using a ¼ glaze. Allow to dry thoroughly, and then, using a scalpel, scratch away some of the colour to create the pale veins.

20 If you want to add some 'caterpillar bites' to the leaves (as in those illustrated), this is done by heating a metal cake tester until it turns red hot, and then piercing the leaf quickly in various places. Because the sugar caramelizes the hole has a brown edge which looks most effective.

SEED PODS

21 Roll a piece of pale green paste into a ball and insert a hooked 24-gauge wire. Pinch the base firmly to secure the paste.

22 Using a scalpel, divide the ball into three (they do not have to be equal parts). Pinch a series of ridges down each section using a pair of tweezers. Insert a fine stamen with the end cut off into the area where the three sections join at the top of the fruit. (This needs to be quite short to represent the pistil.)

23 Dust the ridges to various degrees with a little red and aubergine petal dust. Over-dust the whole thing with spring green. Dip into a full glaze and allow to dry, and then bend the stem into shape.

ASSEMBLY

24 The buds, flowers and leaves are all taped on to one 18-gauge wire to form the main stem. The flowers and buds always come out from a leaf axil, and the leaves alternate down the stem. Tape the whole piece together with ½-width green floristry tape, adding extra wire to support longer stems.

25 Dust the upper surfaces of the main and smaller stems with a mixture of red and aubergine petal dust, and then over-dust the whole thing with dark green and holly/ivy.

Chinese Virginia Creeper

This creeper (*Parthenocissis henryana*) has unusual silvery veins on dull green leaves that turn red during the autumn.

LEAVES

1 Roll out some pale green flower paste using a grooved board. Leave the paste in the groove and place a template on top. Cut around the template using a sharp scalpel.

2 Remove the paste and insert a 26-gauge or 28-gauge wire (depending on the size of the leaf). Place the leaf between the two sides of the appropriate size of veiner, and press firmly. Remove the leaf and place it on a pad. Soften the edge of the leaf using a large celstick. If any of the serrations around the edge are not clear enough, re-cut them using a pair of fine scissors. Allow to dry with a little movement in the edges. Work the base of each leaf between your finger and thumb to fine down and elongate it.

Equipment

Leaf templates (see page 143)
Large, medium and small
hydrangea leaf veiners (GI)
Pale green floristry tape

3 Use the templates to make several different-sized leaves. You will need one large, two medium and two smaller leaves for each group. Make as many groups of leaves as you need, varying the size of group .

COLOURING AND ASSEMBLY

4 Tape the leaves together in groups of three and five. Dust the leaves that will be green first of all with dark green and then holly/ivy. Dust the edge, the base and a little of the central vein on each leaf with

Materials

Pale green flower paste
20, 26, 28 and 30-gauge wires
Holly/ivy, dark green,
aubergine, red, tangerine, skin-tone and white petal dust
(blossom tint)
Silver lustre colour (optional)
Clear alcohol (gin or vodka)
¼ or ½ glaze (see page 10)

aubergine petal dust. The autumnal shades are created using various combinations of tangerine, red, skintone and then aubergine.

5 Using a fine brush, paint in the silvery veins using white petal dust and a touch of green (and silver lustre, if you wish) mixed together with a little clear alcohol. Glaze the leaves using either a ¼ or ½ glaze (depending on your personal taste).

6 Make some tendrils by taping over a 30-gauge wire. Wrap the wire around a paintbrush handle to give it a twisted shape. Make several pieces and tape these together into groups.

7 Tape the various-sized groups of foliage together on to a 20-gauge wire using ½-width green tape. Start with the small groups, and then gradually increase them in size as you work down the stem. Add the tendrils at a leaf axil whenever needed. Bend the whole stem into the required shape, and then dust with the red, aubergine and green colours.

Montbretia

This popular garden hybrid *(Crocosmia)* originates from South Africa although it has also naturalized in Britain and France. It flowers during late summer and early autumn. There are many colour variations, from yellow to very strong reds. Its strong colours make it an ideal flower to use on a man's cake.

Materials

Freesia stamens
Tangerine, red, aubergine,
lemon, moss and dark green
petal dust (blossom tint)
Clear alcohol (gin or vodka)
24, 26 and 30-gauge wires
Melon and pale orange flower
paste

Equipment

White and pale green floristry
tape
Agapanthus cutter (516) or six-
petalled freesia cutters (574,
575, 576)

STAMENS AND PISTIL

1 Paint the ends of three freesia stamens with tangerine and red petal dust mixed with a little clear alcohol or water.

2 To make the pistil, tape over the end of a 30-gauge wire with ¼-width white floristry tape, leaving a small flap of tape at the end. Using a pair of fine scissors, cut the flap into three. Twist each section between your finger and thumb to make quite fine strands.

3 Tape the pistil and stamens together, making the pistil slightly higher. Strengthen the wire by adding a 26-gauge wire. Dust the length of the pistil and the stamens with lemon and tangerine petal dust.

FLOWER

4 Roll a ball of melon-coloured paste into a cone shape. Pinch the broad end of the cone between your fingers and thumbs to thin out the base and form a pedestal shape. Place the flat part of the paste down on the board and roll out using a small celstick. Try to form a tight, neat 'waistline' around the thick area of the pedestal.

5 Cut out the flower using the agapanthus cutter. Before you remove the paste from the cutter, rub your thumb over the paste against the cutter edge to make sure the petals have cleanly cut edges.

6 Place the flower on a board. Broaden each of the petals by rolling with the small celstick. If you want to make a larger flower, elongate the petals as well.

7 Open up the throat of the flower using the pointed end of the celstick. Press the base of each petal against the stick to help form a more graceful shape to the back of the flower.

8 Using the pointed end of a dresden tool, gently draw down a central vein on each petal. Pinch the tip of each petal between your finger and thumb to make a point.

9 Moisten the base of the stamens and pull them down into the centre of the flower. Neaten up the back of the flower and pinch off any excess paste.

COLOURING

10 Dust the flower with tangerine, working from the edges of the petals towards the centre. (Try to keep the centre pale.) Over-dust the edges with red. If you want a slightly darker flower, steam it and then dust it again (see page 10).

BUDS AND BRACTS

11 Attach a small cone of pale orange paste to a 30-gauge wire. Work the base of the cone between your finger and thumb to form a slender bud shape. You will need to make lots of buds in graduating sizes. If you wish you can mark some indents on each bud to represent petals.

12 There are two small bracts at the base of each bud and flower. Cut two small pointed pieces of green paste, vein down the centre, and then attach at the base of the flower or bud. (These can take a lifetime to complete; don't be afraid to leave them off if you haven't got time for them.)

ASSEMBLY

13 Start the stem by taping the smallest bud on to a 24-gauge wire. Continue to add buds down the stem, gradually increasing them in size and working from one side to the other.

14 Before you add the flowers, dust the buds with tangerine and red, leaving the base of each bud much paler. The spray illustrated on page 94 has quite dark buds; to achieve this, mix some red, tangerine and a touch of aubergine with a little clear alcohol, and then paint the colour quite heavily on to the buds.

15 Tape in the flowers, and then dust the base of each and the buds with moss and dark green. Strengthen the stem if needed with more lengths of 24-gauge wire.

Rambling Rose

This rose is based on several different varieties. It has the appearance of an old cottage-garden rose, with its almost untidy flower shape and dusky colour. All the petals are wired individually, which helps to give the finished flower a more irregular look.

Materials

Pale ruby, mid-green and pale green flower paste
18, 24, 26, 28 and 30-gauge wires
Plum, fuchsia, pink, white, lemon, primrose, red, dark green, moss, aubergine and skintone petal dust (blossom tint)
½ glaze (see page 10)

Equipment

Rose petal cutters (278, 277, 276, 551)
Ceramic silk veining tool (HP) or large rose petal veiner (GI)
Pale green floristry tape
Piece of bubble foam
Rose leaf cutters (B6)
Large rose leaf veiner (GI)
Rose calyx cutter (R11b)

FIRST PETAL LAYER

1 Roll out some pale ruby flower paste thinly on a grooved board. Remove the paste from the board and turn it over so that the ridge is on top. Cut out six to ten petals using the smallest cutter (278). Trim some of the petals to make them slimmer. Insert a moistened 30-gauge wire into the central ridge of each petal.

2 Vein each of the petals using either the rose petal veiner or by rolling over the whole surface of each petal with the ceramic silk veining tool. Place the petals on a pad and soften the edges gently using the rounded end of a medium celstick. Cup the centre of each petal and then curl back some of the edges using a cocktail stick (toothpick) and your finger and thumb. It is easier to assemble and tape together these petals before you colour them. Inter-link the petals as you feel they need to be; there is no particular order, except that I tend to use the slimmer petals at the heart of the flower.

REMAINING LAYERS

3 Roll out some more pale ruby paste on a grooved board and cut out approximately five petals using the next size of cutter (277). Insert a 28-gauge wire and vein, soften, cup and curl the edges of each petal as before. Allow to dry over some bubble foam to keep the cupped shape to the petals.

4 For the third layer, repeat step 3 using the next large cutter (276), again cutting out approximately five petals. Allow to dry over the bubble foam until firm enough to handle.

5 The last layer is the same as layers two and three, cutting out the petals using the largest of the cutters (551). Allow to dry as before.

COLOURING

6 Start by dusting the group of petals that are taped together. Colour all over with pink and white petal dust mixed together, then over-dust with plum and fuchsia to make the petals quite dark. The back of each petal should be a little paler.

7 Dust the other petals in paler shades, starting with the pale pink mixture and then over-dusting the centre of each petal on the back and front with the darker pink. Try to keep the edges of the petals much paler. If you are working on a pale-coloured or cream rose, dust a patch of lemon and primrose mixed together at the base of each petal on the back and front.

ASSEMBLY

8 Tape the larger petals around the smaller group that you have already taped, trying to position each petal to hide a join in the previous layer. Gradually tape in the other sizes until you have the size of rose you require. Remember this is a very informal rose with no definite shape. Once the flower has been taped together you can add extra colour if needed to the centre of the flower (the rose can look very flat if there is no depth created by the colouring).

LEAVES

9 I have made the leaves in various sizes and have coloured the smallest to resemble the new growth on each stem. Roll out some pale green paste using a grooved rolling pin or board. Cut out leaves in various sizes using the rose leaf cutters. Remember that the leaves can grow in groups of three or five and that the first leaf is usually larger than the others. For the new-growth foliage I have used the small cutter for all five leaves.

10 Insert a moistened 26-gauge or 28-gauge wire, depending on the size of the leaf. Place each leaf in turn into the double-sided rose leaf veiner and press firmly. Remove the leaf, place on a pad and soften the edges a little with a celstick. Pinch down the central vein, shape the edges and then allow

to firm up for approximately 30 minutes before colouring.

11 Dust the smaller leaves to various depths using plum, skintone, red and aubergine petal dust. Dip into a ½ glaze, shake off the excess, and allow to dry.

12 The larger leaves are dusted with dark green and moss and a little aubergine or plum on the edges. Dust the back of each leaf with white and green petal dust mixed together, and then over-dust areas with aubergine and plum. Dip into a ½ glaze, shake off the excess, and allow to dry.

13 Tape the leaves together into groups of three or five. Start with the largest leaf and then tape two medium leaves below with their stems coming out at the same point. Finish the stem with two of the smaller leaves.

BUDS AND CALYX

14 The buds are made following the instructions on pages 14–15, except this time you will need to make a slightly untidy look when you spiral the petals. Dust them much darker than the flower, and then add a calyx.

15 Roll a ball of mid-green paste into a cone shape and then pinch out the base to form a hat shape. Roll out the paste to make it finer, though the paste should still be quite 'fleshy' when you finish. Cut out the calyx using the rose calyx cutter and then elongate and thin out each sepal using the celstick.

16 Place the calyx on a pad and cup each sepal. Dust the inside of the calyx with a mixture of white and green petal dust to make it paler. If you wish you can make some fine cuts in the edges of each sepal to give them their characteristic 'hairy' appearance. Moisten the centre and attach to the back of the rose or bud, trying to position each sepal so that it covers a join between the outer petals. The calyx would curl right back on a fully open rose, but on the buds it should fit tightly around the petals. Dust with dark green and moss petal dust.

Rue

This wonderful herb *(Ruta graveolens)*, with its beautiful soft blue-green foliage, is a favourite with flower arrangers. It was used during the Middle Ages, together with other herbs and flowers, in a 'tussie-mussie' (posy) to protect against contagious disease. By the sixteenth century, a tussie-mussie was an ornamental gift rather than a medicinal aid.

Materials

Very pale green flower paste
24 and 30-gauge wires
White, dark green, holly/ivy and pearl petal dust (blossom tint)
¼ glaze (see page 10)

Equipment

Triple-spreading E cutters (Zimbabwean cutters)
Pale green floristry tape

1 Roll out some flower paste using a grooved board or rolling pin. Remove the paste from the board, if necessary, and turn it over so that the ridge is on top.

2 Cut out lots of leaves of various sizes using the rue leaf cutters. Before removing the paste from the cutter, rub your thumb over the paste against the cutter edge to make sure the leaf has cleanly cut edges.

3 Insert a moistened 30-gauge wire into almost the full length of the central ridge of each leaf, work the edges with the broad end of a dresden tool, then place the leaf on a pad and soften the edges a little with a small celstick. Cup the back of each leaf with the rounded end of the celstick. Pinch a central vein down each one.

COLOURING AND ASSEMBLY

4 Dust each leaf with a little dark green petal dust. Over-dust with a mixture of holly/ivy and white. If you want to give a very soft effect, add a little pearl dust to the mixture. Dip into a ¼ glaze or steam (see page 10).

5 Tape over each of the stems, and then tape them together in groups of two and three. Tape these smaller stems together on to a 24-gauge wire to form a larger stem. Dust the stems with the soft green mixture and arrange the leaves attractively.

Chinese Witch Hazel

This is the most popular of the witch hazels, originating from western China. This plant *(Hamamelis mollis)* has one of the most exquisite perfumes and is one of my all-time favourites.

Materials

20 and 33-gauge wires
Red/brown flower paste
Aubergine, nutkin and black
petal dust (blossom tint)

Equipment

Yellow, green and beige
floristry tape
Tiny daphne cutter (466)

PETALS

1 Cut some ¼-width strips of yellow floristry tape, and cut several short lengths of 33-gauge wire. Tape over each wire and when you get to the end leave approximately 1.5cm (¾ in) of the tape untwisted. Trim the end, and then vein down the centre using the fine end of a dresden tool. You will need four petals for each flower. Tape the four petals together at the base using ¼-width green floristry tape. (There are some tiny stamens at the centre of the real flower, but it is not essential to include these as they do not affect the overall appearance.)

CALYX

2 Roll a small ball of red/brown paste into a cone, and then pinch the base out to form a hat shape. Place the flat base on a board and thin out using a tiny celstick. Cut out a calyx using the daphne cutter.

3 Open up the centre and mark a vein down the centre of each sepal. Moisten the centre and pull the wired stamens through. Curl the sepals back a little.

4 Dust the calyx and the base of the petals with a little aubergine and nutkin. You will need to make quite a lot of separate flowers to tape together into groups of three or four.

TWIG

5 Start by taping over a 20-gauge wire with beige tape, tapering the end to a slight point. Gradually build up the thickness, adding strips of absorbent kitchen paper where needed to help add bulk. As you work down the twig, tape in the groups of flowers. Join two or three stems together to make a larger piece. Dust with nutkin and a little black dust.

Smoke Tree

There are many cultivated varieties of this wonderful plant *(Cotinus)*. It takes its common name from the tiny flowers, which, from a distance, look like clouds of smoke. The leaves are an excellent choice to add depth to a spray or arrangement, especially during the autumn.

Materials

Pale holly/ivy flower paste
20, 28 and 30-gauge wires
Nutkin, aubergine, deep purple and black petal dust
(blossom tint)

Equipment

Rose petal cutters (276–280)
Poinsettia veiners (GI)
Pale green floristry tape

LEAVES

1 Although the tops of the leaves are very dark purple/brown in colour, their backs are green, which is why green paste should be used. Roll out some paste fairly thinly using a grooved rolling pin or board.

2 Cut out leaves of various sizes using the rose petal cutters. Cut either 30-gauge or 28-gauge wires (depending on the leaf sizes) into five short pieces each. Moisten the end of a piece of wire and insert it into the ridge down the centre of a leaf, inserting the wire to at least half the length of the leaf.

3 Place each leaf between a double-sided poinsettia veiner and press firmly. Remove the leaf and place on a pad. Soften the edges using the rounded end of a celstick or a bone-end tool.

COLOURING

4 Dust the leaves while they are still damp. Dust in layers with nutkin, deep purple, aubergine and black. Steam the leaves when they are a little firmer (see page 10), and then re-dust to achieve a very dark colouring.

5 Tape each stem over with green tape and then group the leaves loosely into clumps, taping them together with ½-width tape. Tape the clumps together on to a stronger stem made from 20-gauge wire.

6 Dust the stems with the same dark mixture used for the leaves.

Snapdragon

This cheerful summer flower (*Antirrhinum majus*) always brings back childhood memories, when I used to squeeze the flowers on both sides to make them 'snap'. There are many colours in the species, but there are also many hybrid forms. They grow mainly with pink, burgundy, white, yellow and orange flowers, although some are bicoloured.

<table>
<tr><td>

Materials

Pale melon and mid-green flower paste
20, 22, 24, 28 and 30-gauge wires
Dark green, lemon and moss petal dust (blossom tint), plus chosen colours
¼ glaze (see page 10)

</td><td>

Equipment

Snapdragon plastic cutting sheet no. 7 (Asi-es)
Ceramic silk veining tool (HP) or metal frilling tool (Asi-es)
Pale green floristry tape
Medium and large stephanotis cutters (567, 566)

</td></tr>
</table>

BOTTOM PETALS

1 Roll out some pale melon paste and place it over the top of the petal shape on the plastic sheet. Roll your rolling pin on top of the paste against the cutting sheet to cut out a petal. Remove the shape and place it flat on a board. Using a metal frilling tool or the ceramic silk veining tool, frill and at the same time vein each of the three petals at the top of the piece.

2 Moisten the edges of the cut-out 'V' shape on either side. Using your fingers, pinch the edges of each 'V' together (this will start to form the characteristic shape). Hollow out the area between the two joined edges using a bone-end tool or medium celstick. Draw down a central vein on this raised area and then pinch a ridge down each side of the vein using a pair of tweezers.

3 Tape over a piece of 22-gauge wire and bend a hook in one end. Moisten the hook and attach a sausage of pale melon paste over it. Moisten the underside and attach to the base petal. Pinch the two pieces together firmly to make sure they are secure. Pinch a ridge on the underside of the petal.

TOP PETALS

4 Roll out some more pale melon paste and cut out as before using the other shaped cutter on the cutting sheet. (I find that this petal is a little large so I usually trim it a little with a pair of fine scissors.)

5 Frill the edges of the two petals, again using either the ceramic silk veining tool or the metal frilling tool. Turn the petal over and mark a 'V' shape on the back using the fine end of a dresden tool. Turn the petal back over and pinch the ridge to

emphasize it a little more. Place the shape on a pad, again with the back of the petal facing up, and cup both of the frilled petals back.

6 Moisten the inside edges of this petal and place on top of the bottom petal. Pinch the two sides together as much as possible, creating quite flat sides to the flower. This is where speed is needed to join the paste as well as possible. Curl back the two petals on the top piece and allow to dry for approximately 30 minutes before colouring with petal dust.

BUDS AND CALYX

7 The small buds are cones of mid-green paste attached to the end of a hooked 28-gauge wire. Mark five indents on the surface to represent unopened petals.

8 The larger buds are made using pale melon paste. Attach a cone of paste to the end of a hooked 24-gauge wire. Pinch two pieces of paste at the top of the cone to represent the two upper petals. Moisten the underside and stick them down. Hollow out the small area between these two petals using the rounded end of the small celstick. Bend the bud so that it is slightly curved.

9 Roll out some mid-green paste thinly and cut out a collection of calyx shapes using either the medium or large stephanotis cutter. Place them on a pad and soften the edges of each of the sepals using the rounded end of a small celstick. Using the fine end of the dresden tool, vein the centre of each sepal. Moisten the calyx and attach to the back of the flower or bud.

COLOURING

10 Dust the raised area on the bottom piece of the flower with lemon petal dust. (Some hybrids have other colours on this part, for example there is a cream form with pink lips!) Dust the rest of the flower with your chosen colour of petal dust, making the back of each flower a little paler. If the colour is not dark enough, steam the flower (see page 10) and re-dust. Dust the calyx with moss and dark green. Allow the flower to dry and then steam to remove the dusty appearance. Leave to dry.

11 Dust the buds using the same colours as the flower, leaving the undersides very pale. (Sometimes the base of the flower has more of the pale melon colour showing.) The tiny green buds are dusted with the same colours as the

calyces on the flowers and larger buds.

BRACTS

12 Behind each of the buds and flowers there is a single bract, that comes out of the base of each short stem. These leaves can be cut out using a small leaf cutter or using a pulled method. I find it easier to attach a tiny cone of paste to the end of a moistened 30-gauge wire. Flatten the paste to make it finer and form the bract shape. Soften the edges if needed and draw down a central vein on each. You will need to make these in graduated sizes to use down the stem. Dust with moss and dark green petal dust. Glaze using a ¼ glaze.

LEAVES

13 The leaves are made in the same way as the bracts using a longer piece of paste on a 30-gauge or 28-gauge wire, depending on the size of the finished leaf. Dust with moss and dark green, making the leaves darker than the bracts. Tape the leaves together to form a small stem using ½-width green floristry tape. You will need a few of these leaf groups to tape on to each stem.

14 Once the flower dies and falls off, it leaves behind the pistil and ovary. To make the pistil, tape over the end of a 30-gauge wire using ¼-width white tape. Leave a flap of tape at the end and cut it in half. Twist each piece between your finger and thumb to make it finer. Dust with the flower colour. For the ovary, attach a ball of green paste at the base of the pistil. Flatten the sides, so that it has three flat, almost triangular-shaped, sides. Add a calyx as for the flower.

ASSEMBLY

15 Start by taping a few of the small green buds on to the end of a 20-gauge wire using ½-width green tape. Attach a couple of the bracts underneath these. Gradually work down the stem, increasing the size of the buds and adding a single bract to each one. When you have achieved enough length with the buds start to introduce the flowers, again taping in a bract at the base of each of the stems. Once you have added your flowers you can start to tape in a pistil and ovary or two, again along with a bract. The last things to tape on to the stem are the groups of leaves. Although a lot of these grow on a stem I usually only give a suggestion of them. Bend the whole of the stem into shape and then dust over the main stem and the smaller stems with the green petal dusts.

Green Hellebore

Hellebores flower during the winter months and included in the family *(Helleborus)* is the ever-popular white Christmas rose. Hellebores have been used in the past to ward off evil spirits and although the plant is highly poisonous it has also been used for various medicinal purposes. If you are planning to work from the real flower, handle with extreme care!

Materials

20, 24, 26 and 28-gauge wires
Tiny white seed-head stamens
Moss, primrose, dark green,
holly/ivy, aubergine, plum,
white and lemon petal dust
(blossom tint)
Pale melon, pale green and
dark green flower paste
Clear alcohol (gin or vodka)
½ glaze (see page 10)

Equipment

Pale green floristry tape
Large stephanotis cutter (566)
Large Christmas rose
cutter (282)
Christmas rose round
veiner (GI)
Horse chestnut leaf
cutters (SC)
Large briar rose leaf
veiner (GI)

PISTIL AND STAMENS

1 To form the pistil, use ¼-width pale green tape. Twist five pieces of tape to make fine strands. Tape these together on to a 28-gauge wire. Curl the tips back a little.

2 Take a good bunch of tiny white seed-head stamens, bend them in half and position them around the pistil so that they are a little shorter. Tape

around the base of the stamens down on to the wire to hold them in place. Colour the tips of the stamens with primrose and lemon petal dust. Dust a little mixed moss and primrose down into the centre to add depth. Dust the tip of the pistil with a touch of aubergine. Curl some of the stamens using a pair of tweezers.

NECTARY (PETALS)

3 These small pieces are actually the flower of this plant; each petal is a nectary. The large 'petals' are actually tepals. Roll out some pale green paste and cut out two shapes using the stephanotis cutter. Place them both on a pad, soften the edges with a celstick, and then draw down a central vein on each using the broad end of a dresden tool. Moisten the base of each petal and then pinch each one together at the base using the tweezers.

4 Moisten the centre of one of the shapes and place the other one on top so that the top petals are in between each of the petals below. Moisten the centre and carefully thread the stamens through the centre. Pinch the paste to secure the flower behind the stamens. Dust with a mixture of moss and primrose petal dust.

TEPALS

5 What appear to be the 'petals' of this flower are actually tepals. Roll out some pale melon paste using a grooved board or rolling pin. Turn the paste over so that the thick ridge is on top, if necessary, and cut out five tepals using the Christmas rose cutter.

6 Insert a moistened 28-gauge wire into each tepal, holding the thick ridge firmly between your finger and thumb. Place each tepal in the double-sided

Christmas rose veiner and press firmly. Remove and place on a pad.

7 Soften the edges using the rounded end of a celstick, and cup the centre slightly. Shape each tepal between your finger and thumb to create a pleasing effect. Allow to dry for approximately 30 minutes.

COLOURING AND ASSEMBLY

8 Mix together moss and primrose petal dust to form a lime green. Dust each tepal from the base on the back and front, leaving the edges much paler. Over-dust the base on the front with a little more moss green. Dust a little aubergine and plum on the edges and at the base on the back of each tepal.

9 Tape the tepals tightly around the stamens and the

flower. Overlap the tepals, if needed, but do not spiral them. Add two 24-gauge wires to the main stem and tape over with ½-width green tape. Holding the stem just behind the flower, bend the wire to form a curve in the stem. Tape two or three small leaves (see below) at the bend in the stem. Dust the stem with aubergine and plum petal dust.

BUDS

10 Attach a cone of pale melon paste on to a taped, hooked 20-gauge wire. Make a 'cage' with five 24-gauge wires (see page 10). Insert the bud, point first, into the 'cage' and close the wires firmly into the paste, keeping them as evenly spaced as possible. While the wires are still in place, pinch the paste out from in between them to form the tepals. Remove the 'cage', and then twist the sections of the bud together to form a neat shape.

11 Dust with the lime green mixture and a little aubergine and plum.

12 Hold the wire behind the bud and bend it to form a curve in the stem. Add a couple of small leaves (see below) at the bend, as for the flower.

LEAVES

13 Roll out some dark green paste using a grooved rolling pin or board. Cut out the leaves either freehand or using the horse chestnut cutters. Insert a 24-gauge or 26-gauge wire (depending on the size of the leaf) into each leaf, inserting the wire to at least half the length of the leaf.

14 Place each leaf in the rose leaf veiner and press firmly. Remove the leaf and place it back on the board. Create a serrated edge using the fine end of the dresden tool, cutting into the edge of the leaf at an angle. Place on a pad and soften the edges a little with a celstick.

15 Pinch the leaf down the centre to reinforce the

vein. Allow to dry over a slight curve. You will need to make one large, two medium and two small leaves for each leaf group required.

16 Dust heavily with dark green, and then over-dust with holly/ivy. Paint a central vein on the leaf using white and a touch of green mixed with a little clear alcohol. Allow to dry and then dip into a ½ glaze, shake off excess, and leave to dry again.

17 Tape the leaves together with ½-width green floristry tape, starting with a large leaf, then adding a medium leaf on either side, and lastly adding two small leaves. Dust the stem with aubergine and plum.

18 Make some smaller leaves in the same way to use behind the flowers and buds. The larger leaves grow at the base of the plant.

Trailing Tropaeolum Cake

The bold colours of nasturtium make it a wonderful subject for a man's birthday cake. I have used it to decorate this very simple cake, allowing the flowers to be the main focus of the design. As this plant attracts a lot of insects it seemed a good idea to include a caterpillar!

Materials

30cm (12 in) long octagonal cake
Apricot glaze
1.5kg (3lb) almond paste (marzipan)
Clear alcohol (kirsch or vodka)
2kg (4lb) sugarpaste, coloured with a little melon and egg yellow paste colouring
Fine willow green ribbon to trim cake
Green satin ribbon to trim board
Nasturtium paste colouring
Dark green, holly/ivy, white, moss, primrose and lemon petal dust (blossom tint)
Pale green flower paste

Equipment

Sugarpaste smoothers
40cm (16 in) long octagonal cake board
Pale green floristry tape
2 posy picks

Flowers

13 nasturtium flowers (see page 88)
11 large and 7 small nasturtium buds (see page 89)
3 nasturtium seed pods (see page 91)
80–90 nasturtium leaves, assorted sizes (see page 90)

PREPARATION

1 Brush the cake with apricot glaze and cover with almond paste. Allow to dry overnight. Moisten the cake with clear alcohol and cover with yellow sugarpaste, using sugarpaste smoothers to achieve a good finish. Cover the cake board with sugarpaste and place the cake on top, making sure there is a neat join between the base of the cake and the board. Allow to dry.

2 Attach a length of willow green ribbon around the base of the cake, and a length of green satin ribbon around the board edge.

PAINTED DESIGN

3 Make a paper pattern from the design on page 141, and scribe it on to the top and sides of the cake. Mix a little clear alcohol with some nasturtium paste colouring and add a touch of white petal dust. Paint in the flower petals using long brush strokes.

4 Dilute some dark green petal dust (again adding a little white), and paint in the leaves and small buds. Paint in the calyces using a mixture of the green dusts and a touch of lemon. Outline any areas of the design if needed using a darker shade of the appropriate colour.

FLOWERS

5 Tape the nasturtiums into loose stems, and then combine together in two groups, one large and one small. Bend the wires of the flowers in the larger spray at an angle of 90° and tape together to form a handle. Insert two posy picks into the cake (one on the top left-hand edge and the other on the right-hand side at the base of the cake). Position the flower sprays into the picks, and then curl and move the stems around to form a pleasing display.

CATERPILLAR

6 To add a bit of fun to the design I have made a tiny green caterpillar using pale green flower paste. Mark the surface of the paste with a scalpel to form the divisions. Dust the caterpillar with moss green and primrose and, before the paste dries, bend it into shape. Attach to the base board using a little egg white.

Cottage Garden Wedding Cake

'Old-fashioned' flowers, like full-blown roses, are currently very popular in bridal bouquets, and here I have combined them with snapdragon in fairly informal sprays. This cake would be particularly suitable for a couple whose wedding reception was to be held in a cottage-style garden.

Materials

20cm (8 in) and 30cm (12 in) oval cakes
Apricot glaze
2kg (4lb) almond paste (marzipan)
Clear alcohol (kirsch or vodka)
3kg (6lb) sugarpaste, coloured with a touch of mint green paste colouring
Fine magenta ('beauty') ribbon to trim cake
Green velvet ribbon to trim board

Equipment

Sugarpaste smoothers
25cm (10 in) and 38cm (15 in) oval cake boards
Celcakes split ring separator
Posy pick

Flowers

TOP
1 large rambling rose and 2 buds (see page 96)
3 pieces of rue (see page 99)
2 large stems of snapdragon (see page 102)
3 stems of large ivy (see page 22)
1 long stem of small rambling rose leaves, plus several shorter stems with larger leaves (see page 97)

MIDDLE
1 large rambling rose,
1 rose bud and 1 half rose (see page 96)
1 main stem of small rose leaves, plus several larger stems (see page 97)

BOTTOM
2 large rambling roses (see page 96)
1 small and 2 large stems of snapdragon (see page 102)
2 large pieces of rue (see page 99)
5 stems of large ivy (see page 22)
Several stems of rambling rose leaves (see page 97)

PREPARATION

1 Brush the cakes with apricot glaze and cover with almond paste. Allow to dry overnight. Moisten the cakes with clear alcohol and cover with pale green sugarpaste, using sugarpaste smoothers to achieve a good finish. Cover the two cake boards with sugarpaste and place the cakes on top, making sure there is a neat join between the base of each cake and its board. Allow to dry overnight.

2 Attach a length of fine ribbon around the base of each cake, and a length of green velvet ribbon around each board edge.

FLOWERS

3 Wire up a small bouquet for the top tier of the cake, following the suggested arrangement on page 112. Make a second, larger, bouquet for the base board, then make a small spray of rambling rose to use on top of the bottom tier to help disguise the cake separator.

4 Place the split ring separator on the centre of the base tier and arrange the small spray of rambling rose inside, positioning part of the rose flower on the outside and part inside. (Some of the leaves and the bud should also be placed on the outside.) Insert a posy pick into the top tier and place the spray in position. (You might find it easier to set the cake up before doing this to get a better idea of where to position the spray.) The larger spray is simply placed next to the base tier with its handle bent to balance the whole piece.

Cottage Garden Spray

This spray has been wired up into an informal version of a reversed 'S' shape. Using a limited number of flowers and plenty of foliage, a spectacular arrangement can still be made. Here the spray is displayed in a coffee pot, perhaps for a wedding table.

Flowers

1 small and 2 large stems of snapdragon (see page 102)
1 large rambling rose and 2 rose buds (see page 96)
1 long stem of small rose leaves, plus several short stems with larger leaves (see page 97)
3 stems of rue (see page 99)
3 stems of large ivy (see page 22)

Equipment

Fine pliers
Pale green floristry tape
Wire cutters
Florists' staysoft

SPRAY

1 To form the basic outline of the spray, bend the ends of the three stems of snapdragon at an angle of 90°, making the smaller stem shorter in length. Tape the three pieces together using ½-width floristry tape. Trim away excess wires.

2 Tape the large rose into the centre to form the focal point, which should be slightly higher than any of the other flowers. Tape in the long stem of small rose leaves, plus a few shorter stems of larger leaves to fill in around the main flower. Add the two rose buds to the left-hand side of the spray.

3 Fill in the large gaps with rue, which will also help to outline the shape of the spray.

4 Tape in the stems of large ivy to complete the spray. Neaten the handle by taping over with floristry tape.

Large Summer Arrangement

This is an extension of the Cottage Garden Spray (page 112), with the addition of several daisies; it could be used to carry the floral theme on to the wedding couple's table. Being large, it is, however, very time-consuming to make.

PREPARATION

1 First of all, strengthen any of the long stems by taping an 18-gauge wire alongside the flower stem. (To support some of the heavier flowers and foliage, you might need a few 18-gauge wires.)

THE ARRANGEMENT

2 Place a clump of staysoft in the pot, making sure it is firmly pressed in.

3 Start by arranging the ivy and rue in the staysoft to form the height and width of the spray. (The height should be at least one and a half times the height of the pot.)

4 Add the snapdragons, using most of them to fill in the gaps in the outline.

5 Use the large roses to fill in the focal area, and add the half roses and buds along with the foliage towards the edges of the arrangement.

6 Finally, add the daisy flowers and buds, spaced around the arrangement, trying to keep it as informal as possible. Add any extra foliage at this stage, if needed, to complete the piece.

Note

The pot used for the arrangement illustrated was one of a pair tied vertically together with rope and string (available from most good florists' shops). I separated the two and, in so doing, was left with a pot with small holes in its sides. I have made good use of one of the holes by inserting a large piece of ivy and a daisy in it at the base of the arrangement.

Scented Winter Arrangement

The hellebores and witch hazel in this arrangement are usually in flower during late winter and I often pick them and bring them indoors, where the scent from the witch hazel soon fills the room.

Flowers

2 twigs of witch hazel (see page 100)
3 hellebore flowers and 2 buds (see page 105)
2–3 sets of hellebore foliage (see page 107)
5 trailing stems of common ivy (see page 122)
3 sets of ivy berries with foliage (see page 123)

Equipment

Florists' staysoft
Silver hot water jug (or similar receptacle)
18-gauge wires
Pale green and beige floristry tape
Fine pliers
Wire cutters
Pewter plate

PREPARATION

1 Place a clump of staysoft in the jug. (If you are worried about damaging the inside of the jug, place the staysoft in a plastic bag before you put it in the jug.) If any of the stems need extra support, tape an 18-gauge wire alongside the main stem.

THE ARRANGEMENT

2 First of all, form the curves of the arrangement by placing the two twigs of witch hazel into the staysoft. Add the two hellebore buds next to the witch hazel. To add depth, add the hellebore foliage next.

3 Add the hellebore flowers, using one of them as the focal point. Try to position the

flower heads so they each face in a slightly different direction. Start to add some of the trailing ivy to form the outline of the piece.

4 Fill in any gaps by threading in the ivy berries and extra foliage. Once everything is in position, stand back and take a look at the arrangement and, if needed, move or 'relax' the flowers a little.

5 To display the arrangement, place it on a pewter plate, which adds balance to the whole piece.

Wild Flowers

WILD FLOWERS have an instant appeal as
they often bring back memories of childhood
summers and Sunday-afternoon walks.
British wild flowers are very understated yet
have a simple beauty that is hard to match.
If this section of the book is slightly shorter
than the first three, it is certainly not for want
of subject matter, but rather because I
covered wild flowers in detail in an earlier
book, and I wanted to devote more of this
book to other types of flowers.

Daisy

The daisy (*Leucanthemum*) has always been a popular subject with flower makers. The only problem with it is that the petals often break when the flowers are being wired into a spray. In this version the petals are all wired individually, making them easier to use.

Materials

20, 22, 28 and 33-gauge wires
White, lemon and pale green flower paste
Lemon, primrose, moss, spring green, dark green and skin-tone petal dust (blossom tint)
¼ glaze (see page 10)

Equipment

Fine pliers
Large-mesh sieve
Narrow daisy petal cutter (613)
Pale green floristry tape
Rose leaf veiner (GI)

CENTRE

1 Bend an 'L'-shaped hook in the end of a 22-gauge wire. Hold the hook halfway down with pliers and curl it back inside itself to form a coil. Bend the whole coil over so that it is at right-angles to the wire and forms a ski-stick shape. Attach a ball of lemon paste to the end and flatten, then allow to dry.

2 Cover the dry paste with another layer of lemon paste. Push the paste against a large-mesh sieve to texture the surface, then indent the centre slightly using the small end of a bone-end tool.

3 Dust the paste with primrose and lemon petal dust. Add a little moss green to the indent in the centre and around the base and edges.

PETALS

4 Roll out some pure white paste on a finely grooved board and cut out lots of petals (you will need approximately 20–30 for each flower).

5 Insert a moistened 33-gauge wire into the very base of the thick ridge down the centre of each petal. Pinch the base firmly to make sure that it is secure.

6 Broaden each petal by rolling with a celstick. Mark several veins on each petal using a dresden tool, and curl the petals a little. Allow to dry for approximately 30 minutes.

7 Tape the petals around the daisy centre using ½-width green tape, leaving a little of the wire showing underneath the centre.

Calyx

8 Roll a ball of pale green paste into a cone shape, and then hollow out the broad end using the rounded end of a small celstick. Moisten the centre, and thread on to the back of the flower. Thin down the back, if needed, and remove any excess paste. To form the scaled effect that the daisy calyx has, press the pointed end of the daisy cutter into the paste many times until the whole calyx is covered.

9 Dust with dark green and a little spring green. Dust the top edge of the calyx at the base of the petals with a little skin-tone petal dust.

Bud

10 Attach a cone of white paste on to a 20-gauge wire, inserting the wire into the pointed end. Indent and slightly cut into the surface using a sharp scalpel to give the impression of unopened petals. Allow to dry, and then add a calyx as for the flower.

Leaves

11 Roll out a small amount of green flower paste using a grooved rolling pin or board. Cut out basic leaf shapes using a scalpel. Insert a 28-gauge wire into at least half the length of each leaf.

12 Cut a serrated edge on each leaf with the scalpel, cutting into the edge and flicking each piece away.

13 Vein the leaves using a rose leaf veiner. Soften the edges with a celstick and shape the whole leaf using your fingers. Pinch down the back of the leaf to reinforce the central vein. Allow to dry for approximately 30 minutes.

14 Dust with spring green and add depth with dark green. Dip into a ¼ glaze, shake off excess, and leave to dry.

15 Tape the leaves alternately down the stem of each bud and flower. Dust the stem with spring green and dark green.

Common Ivy

This form of ivy (Hedera helix) has flowering and non-flowering stems.

Materials

Pale holly/ivy flower paste
20, 26, 28, 30 and 33-gauge
wires
Dark green, moss, aubergine,
primrose, black and holly/ivy
petal dust (blossom tint)
½ glaze (see page 10)
Fine white stamens

Equipment

Ivy cutter/veiners (HH)
Pale green and beige floristry
tape
Common ivy templates (see
page 00)
Large ivy veiners (GI)
Tiny calyx cutter

NON-FLOWERING STEMS

1 The leaves on the non-flowering stems are neat in shape with three to five lobes. Roll out some pale holly/ivy flower paste using a grooved board or rolling pin. Cut out various-sized leaves with the ivy cutter/veiners. Insert a moistened 26-gauge or 28-gauge wire into each leaf, depending on size. Place the leaf on a pad and soften the edges a little with a celstick. Pinch down the centre to make a central vein, and allow to firm up a little before colouring.

2 Dust the leaf while it is still slightly damp, starting with aubergine on the edges. Dust the main part of the leaf with dark green, and then over-dust with holly/ivy. Allow to dry thoroughly.

3 Dip the leaf into a ½ glaze, shake off the excess, and allow to dry. To create the pale veins that the leaf has, scratch away some of the glaze and colour, and actually scratch into the sugar, following and adding to the main veins on the paste.

4 Tape the leaves on to a 26-gauge wire using ½-width beige tape. You can start the stem with a tendril if you wish, but on real ivy this tends to be a very small leaf forming. The size of leaf varies on each stem, and sometimes two leaves develop at the same point.

FLOWERING STEMS

5 The leaves on flowering stems are made in exactly the same way as for non-flowering stems, except that they are cut out with large, heart-shaped leaf templates made from the outlines on page 142. Vein with the large ivy veiner. Use a heavier gauge of wire, and when you colour the leaf use less aubergine petal dust and a little moss green as well as the other two greens to make a brighter leaf colour. Glaze and scratch as before.

FLOWERS AND BUDS

6 Cut a length of 33-gauge wire into short pieces and bend a tiny hook on each. Attach a tiny ball of green paste to the end and insert five tiny white stamens. Allow to dry.

7 Roll out a small piece of paste, leaving the centre slightly thicker. Cut out a calyx shape using the tiny calyx cutter. Place it on a pad and stretch each petal using strong strokes with a small celstick. Moisten the centre and pull the stamens through so that the two fit tightly together. Curl the petals back. You will need to make a lot of these flowers to make up a flower head.

8 Dust the centre of each flower with moss green and primrose mixed together. Tape a collection together with the stems all coming out at the same point.

9 To make the buds, attach a tiny ball of paste to a hooked 33-gauge wire. Mark some indents on the surface to give the impression of unopened petals. Tape buds together in clusters.

BERRIES

10 Cut short lengths of 30-gauge wire. Roll a ball of green paste and insert the wire so that it almost comes out at the other end, forming a sharp point. Pinch the point if it is not sharp enough. Using a pair of tweezers, pinch five lines around the top part of the berry to form a pentagon shape.

11 Tape over each stem with ¼-width green tape. Dust the berries to various degrees of ripeness, using a little aubergine and black to colour the top part of each berry, and moss green on the sides. The more mature the berry, the blacker it should be. Tape the berries into clusters and steam (see page 10) to take away the dusty appearance.

ASSEMBLY

12 Start a stem with either a cluster of buds, flowers or berries, and then tape in a small leaf. Work down the stem, adding larger leaves and a 20-gauge wire to add bulk. Dust the stem with the green petal dust. Add other clusters and smaller stems to the main one if you wish.

Columbine

Often called 'granny's bonnet', the columbine (*Aquilegia vulgaris*) can have dark purple, pale violet/pink or white flowers. These plants were once used to cure sore throats, which is very strange as they are highly poisonous! They are, however, one of the most attractive flowers during the late spring and early summer months.

Materials

Fine white stamens
20, 24, 28 and 30-gauge wires
Bluebell, lavender, cornflower blue, violet, dark green, vine green, plum and primrose petal dust (blossom tint)
Pale melon and pale holly/ivy flower paste
¼ glaze (see page 10)

Equipment

Pale green floristry tape
Fine pliers
Daisy petal cutter (89)
Ceramic silk veining tool
Rose calyx cutter (R11b)
Oak leaf geranium cutters
Frilled geranium cutter
Aquilegia leaf veiner (GI)

STAMENS

1 Bend a group of fine white stamens in half and tape alongside a 24-gauge wire. Dust the tips of the stamens with primrose, and then curl back some of the tips using pliers. Dust the centre of the stamens with a little vine green.

PETALS

2 Each of the petals is formed in a tubular shape.

Roll out some pale melon paste and cut out five petals using the daisy petal cutter. Roll with the veining tool to broaden and vein.

3 Using a cocktail stick (toothpick) to support the petal, roll it into a tubular shape. If the paste starts to dry out use a little egg white to stick the two edges together. Roll the base of the petal very finely between your finger and thumb. Thin the upper edge of the petal by frilling with a cocktail stick. Curl the fine base into shape. Allow to dry a little before colouring.

TEPALS

4 Roll a ball of pale melon paste into a cone shape and then pinch around the base to form a hat shape. Roll out the

paste around the thick area at the centre, still leaving the paste quite 'fleshy'. Cut out the shape using the large rose calyx cutter.

5 Divide the calyx shape into five separate pieces using a sharp scalpel. Insert a moistened 30-gauge wire into the base of each tepal. Roll the base of each tepal between your finger and thumb to make it finer. Broaden and vein at the same time using the ceramic silk veining tool. Place each of the tepals on the pad and soften the edges. Curl the base of each of the tepals back and give the tips a sharp pinch. Allow to firm up.

COLOURING AND ASSEMBLY

6 Dust each of the petals and tepals with a mixture of equal proportions of bluebell and lavender. Add depth by dusting into the tubes, at the base of the petals and down the centre on both sides of the tepals using a mixture of cornflower blue and violet.

7 Tape the tepals around the stamens using ½-width pale green floristry tape. To stick the petals in place you will need to mix up a glue; mix a little egg white with some flower paste and work it with the broad end of a dresden tool to form a smooth paste. Apply a little of this glue to the base of the stamens in between the tepals. While the glue is still wet, position the five petals in between the tepals.

8 Tape a length of 20-gauge wire on to the main stem to make it both longer and stronger.

9 For a seed-head, insert a 30-gauge wire into the base of a teardrop-shaped piece of pale holly/ivy paste, pinch a ridge down one side with your finger and thumb, thin down the tip to make it very fine, and curl as illustrated. Make another four, and then tape together with the curled tips on the outside, using ¼-width tape. Dust with plum, vine and dark green.

LEAVES

10 Roll out some holly/ivy paste using a grooved rolling pin or board. Cut out one large and two small leaves using a combination of the two sizes of oak leaf geranium and the frilled geranium cutters. Insert a moistened 28-gauge wire into almost the full length of each leaf. Vein using the aquilegia leaf veiner.

11 These leaves are actually quite flat on the edges, but I prefer to give them more movement. Work on the edge using the broad end of the dresden tool. Pinch the leaf down the centre and allow to dry a little before colouring.

12 Dust the edges with plum. Colour the main part of the leaf with dark green, and then over-dust with vine green. Dip into a ¼ glaze, shake off excess, and leave to dry.

13 Tape the leaves together into threes using ½-width green tape.

Oak

The best known and most loved tree in Britain is without doubt the majestic oak
(Quercus). Oak is always a good piece to use on a man's birthday cake, a
retirement cake, or even on an autumn wedding cake.

Materials

Cream and pale green flower
paste
26 and 28-gauge wires
Dark green, skintone,
holly/ivy, tangerine, lemon,
nutkin, cream, moss and black
petal dust (blossom tint)
¼ and ¾ glazes (see page 10)

Equipment

Oak leaf cutters
Oak leaf veiners (GI)
Nutmeg grater
Brown floristry tape

LEAVES

1 Decide whether you want
leaves in autumn colours or
green. If you plan to make
autumn leaves, then it is better
to work with cream flower
paste. Roll out some paste using
a grooved rolling pin or board,
and cut out leaves using various
sizes of oak leaf cutters.

2 Insert a moistened 26-gauge
or 28-gauge wire (depending
on the size of the leaf), making
sure the wire is inserted to at
least half the length of the ridge.
Place each leaf into an oak leaf
veiner and press firmly.

Remove the leaf, place it on a
pad and soften the edges with a
celstick. Allow to dry for
approximately 30 minutes.

COLOURING

3 Dust the leaves to various
depths of colour. Start dusting down the centre of each leaf
with dark green, holly/ivy and
moss. Dust in from the edge of
each leaf with cream, lemon,
tangerine, skintone and nutkin
(try to give variation in your
colouring). Dip each leaf into a
¼ glaze, shake off the excess,
and leave to dry.

ACORNS

4 Roll a ball of cream flower
paste into an acorn shape
(quite straight sides with a
rounded top). Insert a hooked,
moistened 26-gauge wire into
the base. Pinch a tiny sharp
point at the tip. Mark the sides
of the nut using a scriber or the
back edge of a scalpel. (These
long markings should be very
light and straight, continuing
down to the base of the nut.)
Dust the nut with cream, tangerine and a little moss green.
Dip the acorn into a ¾ glaze,
shake off the excess, and allow
to dry.

5 To make the acorn cup, use a smaller piece of green paste. Roll into a ball, and then hollow out using the rounded end of a celstick. Thin out the edges of the cup by pressing them against the sides of the celstick. Leave the tool in the cup and roll the sides of the paste against a nutmeg grater to give a textured surface.

6 Moisten the centre of the cup and attach to the base of the acorn, making sure that it fits neatly. Pinch off any excess paste. Dust the cup with cream, moss, nutkin and a little black in places. Make some extra cups, but this time insert a moistened 26-gauge wire into the base of each one. Quite often the nut has fallen off and it looks interesting in a spray if you have the odd cup in amongst the full acorns. Dust the inside of the cup a dark cream/brown, leaving a pale area at the centre. Paint with ¾ glaze and allow to dry.

7 Sometimes there are some tiny brown nuts at the base of the larger ones. These are made in the same way as before, colouring them with nutkin and a little black.

Assembly

8 Tape two or three acorns, with or without empty cups, very tightly together at the base. Add the smaller nuts as required, again keeping them tight in with the other nuts. Tape a group of leaves in various sizes behind each clump of nuts.

Notes

Both the shape of the acorn and the oak foliage vary from one species of oak to another. There are many species; though often thought of as a traditionally British tree, only two species of oak are native to Britain – the sessile and the English oak. The oak is a common sight in parks and large gardens, where it supplies a habitat and food source to many animals, birds and insects.

Medlar

Medlar (*Mespilus germanica*) is a shrub that has quite small flowers and huge green-brown apple-like fruits. It makes quite an unusual and interesting subject to use on a cake, either by itself or with other autumn fruits in a large arrangement. Because the fruit is very large I have scaled it down to make it more suitable to use on a cake.

Stamens

1 Take a group of stamens and bend them in half. Tape a short length of 26-gauge wire alongside using ¼-width green floristry tape. Open up the stamens a little using tweezers. If using white stamens, paint the tips with a mixture of alcohol and nutkin petal dust. Allow to dry, and then dust in the centre with a mixture of primrose and moss green.

Petals

2 Roll out some white flower paste thinly using a grooved rolling pin or board. Cut out five petals with the heart-shaped cutter. Cut five short lengths of 30-gauge wire, moisten the end of each and insert into the thick ridge of each petal.

3 Frill the edges using the broad end of a dresden tool, or work them with a cocktail stick (toothpick). Cup the centre of each petal with the small end of a bone-end tool. Pinch the base and then curl back the

edges of each petal. Allow to
dry slightly over a gentle curve.

4 Dust the base of each petal
with a mixture of primrose
and moss green. Dust the whole
of each petal with champagne
petal dust.

5 Tape the petals evenly
around the stamens. If the
petals are still damp you can
now gently re-shape the edges
if needed.

CALYX

6 Roll a ball of green flower
paste into a teardrop shape
and pinch out the base to form a
hat shape. Roll out the base
using a small celstick. Cut out
the shape using the largest rose
calyx cutter (248). Vein and
pinch down the centre of each
sepal, forming the tip into a
long, sharp point. Dust the
inside of the calyx with white
and moss green petal dust.

7 Moisten the centre of the
calyx and position it on to

the back of the flower, trying to
cover a join in the petals with
each of the sepals. Curl the tips
of each sepal back. Dust the
back of the calyx with dark
green and moss.

BUD

8 Roll a cone of white paste
and insert a hooked, moistened 26-gauge wire into the
broad base. Using a 'cage' made
from five 30-gauge wires (see
page 10), indent the bud to give
the impression of unopened
petals. Pinch the tip into a sharp
point. Add a calyx as for the
flower using one of the smaller
cutters (this will depend on the
size of the bud). Dust the calyx
as for the flower.

FRUIT

9 Roll a large ball of brown
flower paste. Flatten it slightly. Roll out some more of the
brown paste and cut out a shape
using one of the smaller calyx
cutters. Moisten the back of the

calyx and place on to the surface
of the ball. Using the pointed
end of a celstick, embed the
shape into the ball. Open up the
centre a little more and then
insert a taped, hooked and
moistened 20-gauge wire, making sure the hook is hidden
inside the fruit.

10 Texture the surface of the
fruit by rolling over with
a styro-foam ball. Make fruit in
various sizes for each branch.

11 Dust the whole of each
fruit with nutkin brown
petal dust. Shade in areas and
add depth to the centre of the
fruit using some more nutkin
mixed with black. To add a
mossy effect dust in places with
spring green. Dip into a ¼ glaze,
shake off excess, and leave to
dry. You might find the fruit
needs dusting gently again after
glazing to give a denser appearance.

LEAVES

12 Roll out some mid-green
paste using a grooved
rolling pin or board. Cut out the
leaves using a sharp scalpel
(these vary in size and are oval
in shape with a point at the
end). Insert a moistened 26-
gauge wire into the central
ridge to at least half the length
of each leaf.

13 Vein using the large rose leaf veiners (you will need the Asi-es veiner for the very large leaves). Place on a pad and soften the edges using a large celstick. Pinch the leaves down the centre and dry over a gentle curve until firm enough to dust.

14 Dust the edges of each leaf to various degrees with lemon, tangerine, skintone and nutkin brown. Colour the main body of the leaf with dark green, moss and holly/ivy. Dip the leaves, one at a time, into a ½ glaze, shake off excess, and leave to dry.

ASSEMBLY

15 Tape a group of leaves behind each flower and fruit using ½-width brown floristry tape. Arrange these together to form a branch, adding extra leaves as needed. Dust the branches with nutkin brown and a little black.

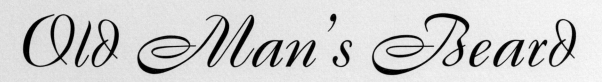

Old Man's Beard

This plant (*Clematis vitalba*) is a member of the large Clematis family. 'Old man's beard' is the name given to the hairy seed-heads that the plant produces in autumn.

Materials

White silk thread
24, 28 and 33-gauge wires
Lemon, moss, primrose, dark green, aubergine, skintone and nutkin petal dust (blossom tint)
Holly/ivy flower paste
½ glaze (see page 10)

Equipment

Pale green floristry tape
Simple leaf cutters (225-232)
Clematis montana veiner (GI)

SEED-HEADS

1 Wrap some silk thread around two parted fingers eight times. Remove from your fingers and twist the loop into a figure-of-eight shape, then bend the shape in half to form a smaller loop. Thread a 33-gauge wire though the centre of the loop of silk, bend it over the thread, and tape over the base of the silk and down on to the wire using ½-width tape.

2 Cut the silk and open it up. Dust the very centre with nutkin petal dust to represent the seeds. Moisten the centre and the very tips of the thread with egg white, then pull back the silk and twist the ends around the wire. Allow to dry, and then tease the silk open again. (The egg white will stiffen the silk to hold it in position.) Dust with lemon.

LEAVES

3 Roll out green paste using a grooved board. Cut out different-sized leaves using the leaf cutters. The leaves grow in groups of three or five, the top leaf tending to be larger, so for each group you will need one large leaf and two or four smaller ones.

4 Insert a moistened 28-gauge wire into each leaf.

Vein with the clematis veiner, then make cuts in the edges with scissors.

5 Dust the leaves with moss and primrose, adding depth with dark green. Dust the edges with aubergine. Glaze using a ½ glaze. Tape the leaves together in groups.

6 Tape over each of the stems with ¼-width green tape. Group the seed-heads in separate stems of two and three. Tape the leaves and seed-heads on to a main stem (24-gauge wire), noting that the leaves grow with two sets opposite each other. Dust the stems with aubergine and skintone.

Lazy Daisy and Busy Bee

Daisies are a wonderful subject for a summer birthday cake. The flowers could also be wired up as a daisy chain and displayed around the base of the cake, and if the bumble-bees are not to your taste, there is an alternative brush embroidery design on page 143.

Materials

20cm (8 in) long octagonal cake
Apricot glaze
750g (1½lb) almond paste (marzipan)
Clear alcohol (kirsch or vodka)
1kg (2lb) white sugarpaste
Fine willow green ribbon to trim cake
Green velvet ribbon to trim board
Holly/ivy, dark green and white petal dust (blossom tint)
Royal icing (optional)

Equipment

Sugarpaste smoothers
30cm (12 in) long octagonal cake board
Bumble-bee ink stamp
Green floristry tape

Flowers

5 daisies and 4 buds (see page 120)

PREPARATION

1 Brush the cake with apricot glaze and cover with almond paste. Leave to dry overnight. Moisten the almond paste with clear alcohol and cover with sugarpaste, using smoothers to achieve a good finish.

2 Cover the cake board with sugarpaste, and place the cake on top, making sure you have a neat join between the base of the cake and the board. Allow to dry for 2 days.

3 Attach a length of fine green ribbon around the base of the cake, and a length of velvet ribbon around the board edge.

SIDE DECORATION

4 The bumble-bee design is created using an ink stamp that I bought from a National Trust shop. Mix together holly/ivy, dark green and white petal dust on a saucer with a little clear alcohol, to form a fairly thick consistency. Apply the colour to the ink stamp using a broad paintbrush (trying not to paint too much on to the surface of the stamp as this will make the design smudge on the cake surface). Press the stamp in the desired places, using a firm press-and-release motion. To give the cake a little humour, if desired, paint a series of 'Z's above the bumble-bees. Use the green paint mixture again and a very fine paintbrush.

THE SPRAY

5 This is probably the easiest spray I have ever put together! Simply bunch the flower and bud stems attractively, and fasten together at one point using ½ -width floristry tape. Rest the flowers diagonally across the cake surface. If you wish to secure the spray, pipe a little royal icing under the stems.

Autumnal Fruit and Nut Cake

This unusual design would be ideal for a birthday cake. The cake has an interesting texture; along with the oak, ivy fruit and seed-heads of old man's beard, it gives it quite a rustic look.

Materials

20cm (8 in) heart-shaped cake
Apricot glaze
750g (1½ lb) almond paste
(marzipan)
Clear alcohol (kirsch or vodka)
1kg (2lb) sugarpaste, coloured
with holly/ivy paste colouring
Dark green, holly/ivy and tangerine petal dust (blossom
tint)
Pearl and pastel green lustre
colours
Green velvet ribbon to trim
board

Equipment

Sugarpaste smoothers
30cm (12 in) heart-shaped cake
board
Large and small hydrangea
leaf veiners
Round-headed grooved cocktail sticks (toothpicks)
Posy pick

Flowers

1 large and 1 small Autumnal
Spray (see page 137)

PREPARATION

1 Brush the cake with apricot glaze and cover with almond paste. Leave to dry overnight. Moisten the almond paste with clear alcohol and cover with green sugarpaste, using sugarpaste smoothers to achieve a good finish. Cover the cake board with sugarpaste, and place the cake on top, making sure you have a neat join between the base of the cake and the board.

DESIGN

2 Using the ridged side of the hydrangea leaf veiners, emboss the cake's surface in the desired areas. Mark some stems on the cake with the fine end of a dresden tool to link the foliage together. Once the leaf design is completed, texture the whole surface of the cake and board with the rounded ends of a bunch of grooved cocktail sticks (toothpicks). The surface of the cake then becomes recessed, while the leaf design stands proud.

3 Dust the leaf design with variations of dark green, holly/ivy and tangerine, and then over-dust with the lustre colours. Dust around the base of the cake with a mixture of dark green and holly/ivy.

4 Attach a length of velvet ribbon around the edge of the board.

5 Wire up the sprays as described on page 137, and position on the cake. The large spray should be inserted into a posy pick pushed into the top left-hand corner of the cake, while the small spray simply rests on the cake board.

Autumnal Spray

There are two sprays on the Autumnal Fruit and Nut Cake (page 134); the instructions given here are for the larger one. The smaller spray is simpler in form, the flowers simply being taped together at one point.

Large spray

6 pieces of oak, plus extra foliage (see page 126)
3 stems of old man's beard (see page 131)
3 pieces of berried common ivy with foliage (see page 122)
1 piece of flowering common ivy with foliage, plus 2 clusters of ivy buds (see page 122)

Small spray

2 stems of non-flowering ivy foliage (see page 122)
1 clump of oak with acorns (see page 126)
1 clump of oak without acorns (see page 126)
3 clumps of ivy berries (see page 123)
2 flowering ivy stems (see page 122)
1 stem of old man's beard foliage (see page 131)

Equipment

24-gauge wires
Green floristry tape
Fine pliers
Wire cutters

1 To strengthen all the stems, tape on additional lengths of 24-gauge wire using ½-width floristry tape. Decide on the size and shape of the spray and then gather together five stems (here I have used three pieces of oak and two stems of old man's beard). Bend each stem to an angle of 90°, and then tape them together using ½-width floristry tape. This will form a handle to the spray.

2 Add the focal point in the centre of the spray. In this case I have used a clump of oak. Add another two clumps of oak to fill the gaps around the centre.

3 Finally, tape in the ivy berries, flowers and foliage, spacing them mainly around the focal point. Cut off any excess wire from the handle to cut down on the bulk, and tape over with full-width tape to neaten.

4 For the smaller spray, simply gather the pieces together attractively and tape at one point.

Granny's Bonnet Birthday Cake

'Granny's bonnet' is yet another common name for aquilegia, so it is an obvious choice for a grandmother celebrating her birthday during late spring or early summer!

Materials

20cm (8 in) oval cake
Apricot glaze
750g (1½ lb) almond paste (marzipan)
Clear alcohol (kirsch or vodka)
1kg (2lb) champagne sugarpaste
Cream and white (optional) royal icing
Soft pine ribbon to trim board
Violet, lavender and deep purple petal dust (blossom tint)

Equipment

Sugarpaste smoothers
30cm (12 in) oval cake board
Crimper
Nos. 0 and 42 piping tubes (tips)
Thick card
A4 plastic file pocket
Florists' staysoft
Small cake card
Glue gun and non-toxic glue stick

Flowers

8 aquilegia flowers and 5 buds (see page 124)
3–5 aquilegia seed-heads (see page 125)
Many clumps of aquilegia foliage (see page 125)

PREPARATION

1 Brush the cake with apricot glaze and cover with almond paste. Leave to dry overnight. Moisten the almond paste with clear alcohol, and cover the cake with sugarpaste, using sugarpaste smoothers to achieve a good finish.

2 Cover the cake board with sugarpaste, and crimp the edge. Place the cake on the board. Allow to dry.

3 Pipe a shell border around the base of the cake using cream-coloured royal icing and a piping bag fitted with a no. 42 piping tube. Attach a length of ribbon to the edge of the board.

SIDE DECORATION

4 Trace the leaf design on page 143 several times on to a piece of tracing paper. Cut a piece of thick card to fit into an A4 plastic file pocket, and insert it, with the tracing paper, into the pocket so that the traced design shows through.

5 Pipe over the lace work, using white or cream royal icing and a piping bag fitted with a no. 0 piping tube. Allow the lace to dry, and then colour each piece while it is still on the file pocket using first of all violet and then a mixture of lavender and deep purple petal dust.

6 Scribe a fine line on to the cake, either freehand or using a template, to help position the embroidery and lace. Pipe the embroidery just above the scribed line using a no. 0 piping tube. (This piping can be piped freehand, or you can trace the embroidery design from page 143, scribe it on to the cake, and then pipe over it.) Using the pointed end of a cel-stick, create the eyelet holes and then pipe around the edge of each one. Allow to dry, and then petal dust over the embroidery with appropriate colours.

7 Attach the lace to the cake with royal icing, piping two tiny dots on to the cake's surface for each piece of lace, and gently holding the lace in position until it will stay in place.

FLOWERS

8 Attach a lump of florists' staysoft to the small cake card using a glue gun. Arrange the flowers in the staysoft, trying to make the display quite informal. You might find bending the base of each wire into a hook before inserting it into the staysoft will help to hold the stems a little more firmly. Remember to reserve one stem to place on the other side of the cake to complete the design.

Templates

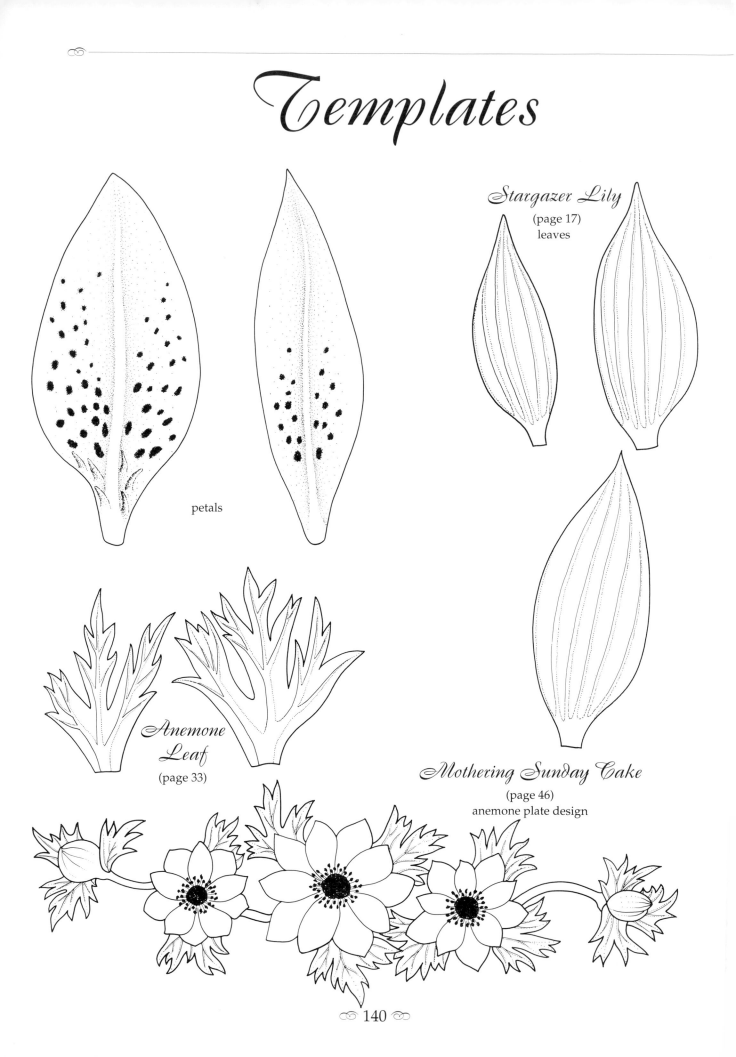

petals

Stargazer Lily
(page 17)
leaves

Anemone Leaf
(page 33)

Mothering Sunday Cake
(page 46)
anemone plate design

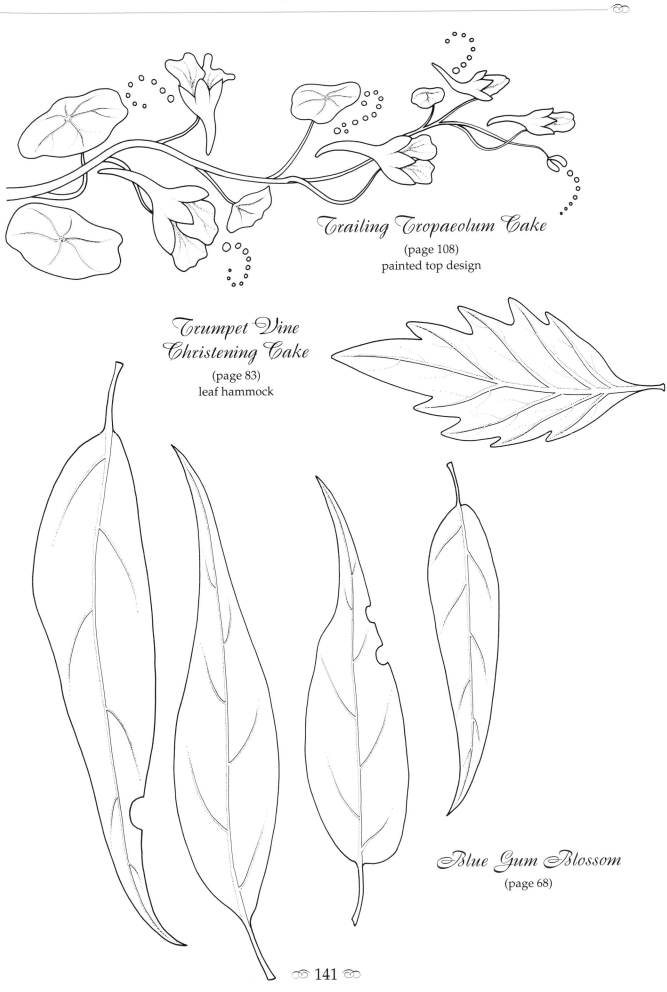

Trailing Tropaeolum Cake
(page 108)
painted top design

Trumpet Vine
Christening Cake
(page 83)
leaf hammock

Blue Gum Blossom
(page 68)

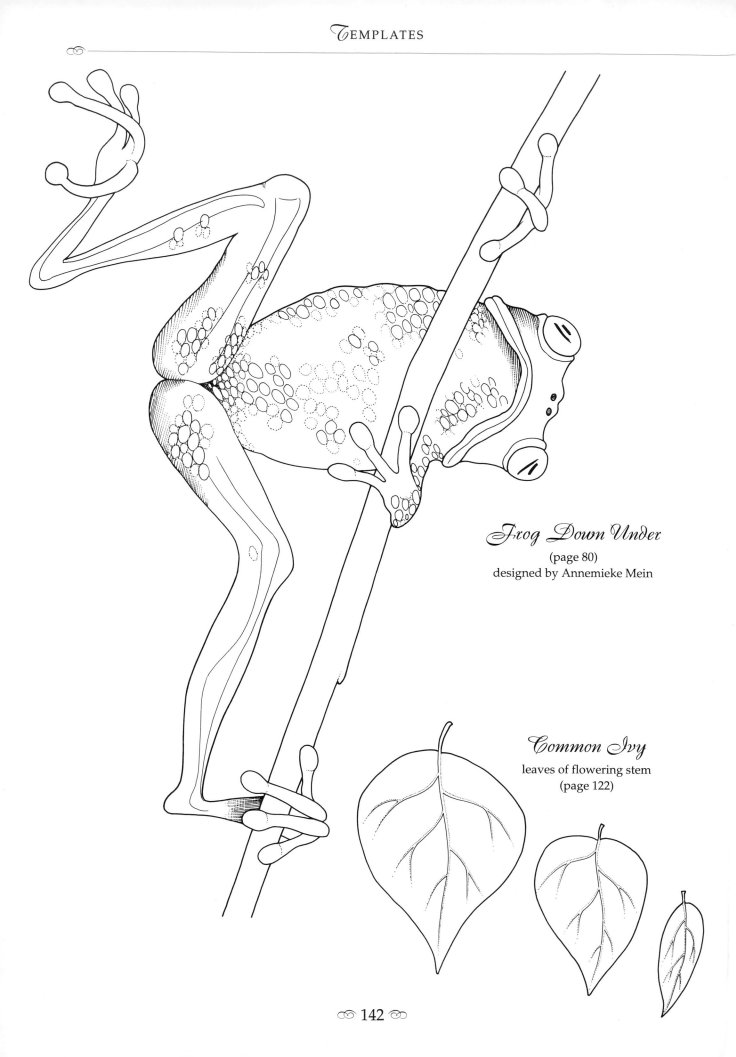

Frog Down Under
(page 80)
designed by Annemieke Mein

Common Ivy
leaves of flowering stem
(page 122)

Lazy Daisy and Busy Bee

(page 132)
daisy embroidery design

Chinese Virginia Creeper

(page 92)

Granny's Bonnet Birthday Cake

(page 138)
lace leaf and embroidery